Upfront Financing in the Digital Age

Funding Advice to the World's
56,000,000 Current Start-Ups

David Silver

Copyright: David Silver, 2016.
    All Rights Reserved.

Cover Photo Copyright: FamZoo Staff, 2010.
    Used under the Creative Commons License.
    Retrieved from www.flickr.com.

Published by CD Jervis Literary, Inc.
    4001 Office Court Drive, Suite 604
    Santa Fe, NM 87507

In Memoriam

Michael E. Timm

I am grateful to Chris Nierman and Scott Chumpelik for assisting me in creating "Upfront Financing in the Digital Age," and to Claude and Caleb Silver with their digital marketing advice.

David Silver Santa Fe, NM July, 2016

Table of Contents

INTRODUCTION 1

FINDING A PROBLEM IN SEARCH OF A SOLUTION 9

STUDYING THE PROBLEM VIA DEEP GOOGLING AND OTHER SEARCH SITES 16

MEASURING THE SIZE OF THE OPPORTUNITY 23

WILL YOUR NEW BUSINESS IDEA SUCCEED? 30

PROVIDING ANSWERS TO THE FIVE MAIN QUESTIONS SMART INVESTORS ASK 42

WRITING THE BUSINESS PLAN/FUNDING MEMORANDUM 56

SOURCES OF UPFRONT FINANCING 62
    Family and Friends: 62
    Angel Clubs: 63
    Angel Capital Funds: 67
    Kickstarter, SeedInvest and Other Online Funding Sources: 69
    Licensee Money: 78
    Vendor Money: 82
    Purchase Order Financing: 84
    Venture Capital Funds With Seed Capital Divisions: 86
    Strategic Funding Sources: 88
    Grants and 501-C3 Buddy Cars: 91
    Leveraged Buyouts: 96
    Business Development Corporations 120
    State Funding Programs 122
    Small Business Investment Companies 125
    Reverse Merger Into Public Shells 126
    SPACs – Special Purpose Acquisition Companies 128

INTRODUCTION

"It ain't braggin' if you've done it," Joe Namath was alleged to have said. So, it ain't braggin' when I tell you that I have raised more upfront financing for more entrepreneurs than any other person on the planet over the last 50 years. I estimate my totals at 350 entrepreneurial companies, for which I have raised $1.2 billion. It is difficult to count the jobs that I have helped to create, but it is somewhere around 2,000,000. I was working as a young associate in the legendary investment bank, Kuhn Loeb & Co., back in 1967 when two young men, Bill Hambrecht and the late George Quist, came into the office and asked the partners to raise $6,000,000 for them to start something called a venture capital fund. Because I was the only person in the firm who could program a computer, a special gift given to me by the University of Chicago Graduate School of Business in my last class in 1963, the partners sent me all of the technology entrepreneurs that knocked on our door. There were not very many. The Kuhn Loeb partners' wealth came from funding the railroads, the advent of electricity, rebuilding Japan after World War II, Bethlehem Steel, Copperweld, Uniroyal and industrial companies of that ilk. They had never heard the word "software," for instance and computers were giant IBMs with much less storage and speed than today's smartphones. But, I knew that software was more important than hardware, just by counting how few automobile makers there were versus the ubiquity of oil and gas producers. One of the keys to success in business, I have found, with my many losses, is low COGs – low Cost of Goods Sold – and software has that marvelous feature. Social networks have no COGs, which means buckets of cash flow coming down to Operating Expenses, which are more controllable than COGs.

Bill and George literally got on their knees in the genuflecting position and begged me to "green light" their deal – which I did, with zero confidence in my decision. But, as it turned out, I was right. Bill Hambrecht is one of the most successful venture capitalists and investment bankers in the world. And, they came back two years later with quite a few successes in their portfolio and asked the partners to raise $20,000,000 for their combined investment bank and venture capital fund. I worked on that raise as well.

But, to learn how wealth was created, it would take a couple of different entrepreneurs. First was Vince Wolfington, whom I met when I trained at Chase Manhattan Bank, my first employer, from 1964 to 1967. He was in the credit department, along with me and another 50 or so young men. Vince came to Kuhn Loeb & Co., where I had moved in 1967, and asked me to raise $2.5 million for the purchase of Chevway Corporation, a small publicly-held company that was helping Chevrolet dealers segue into the automobile leasing business. The partners put up the money this time, and did not syndicate it to their "angel investing group," although it was not called that as that esteemed group included the Crown Agents' money, i.e., the Royal Family of Great Britain. Chevway was riskier than a Philippe Petit high wire walk. But, to our shock and surprise, the stock price shot up from $2.00 to $50.00 a share, and after a 10-day battle with my boss, Harvey M. Krueger, I was rewarded with 5,000 shares by the partners. When the Securities & Exchange Commission permitted us to sell our shares, my wife and I had $250,000 in our cash account, which was much more than my salary of $10,000 and her teacher's salary of $5,000. And that is how I learned how wealth was created – I would back entrepreneurs for the rest of my life. But, first we used some of the money to buy a 14-room home on twelve and one-half acres in the Hudson Valley.

The second wealth creator was Automatic Data Processing, Inc., known as "ADP," and I visited them above an A&P in Clifton, NJ. The father of Henry Taub, one of the founders of ADP, was an accountant in the garment district in New York City. He told Henry that employees were going home on Fridays without a paycheck because the accounting departments could not figure out how to deduct FICA, FUTA and SUTA, the deductions that the Internal Revenue Service and state taxing agencies were sending to employers to collect taxes for them. ADP would write the software to handle this job for employers. Frank Lautenberg, another founder of ADP, and later to become a U.S. Senator for New

Jersey, asked Harvey if he could borrow me for a while. Frank and I traveled the country acquiring key punch operators so that ADP could avoid opening data processing operations in myriad cities.

So brilliant was Frank, that he created an association before we headed out on our journey. It was called ADAPSO, the Association of Automatic Data Processing Service Organizations. I bought the Yellow Pages of fifteen large cities, and telephoned the owners of the key punch operators in those cities, and invited them to meet Frank and me for dinner to discuss their joining ADAPSO. We made a dozen acquisitions with ADP stock. One night in San Diego following dinner, Frank stood up to speak and he talked about ADP's desire to make acquisitions of the leading key punch operators on major cities. I noticed a white cloth napkin had been passed up to me by a woman sitting across from me who owned Mail Me Monday, Inc. She had written in ink her basic revenue and earnings numbers as well as some balance sheet figures.

What I learned as ADP's de facto business development officer, was how wealth was created with leverage. The leveraged buyout was just beginning to be used by buyers to use the assets and cash flow sellers to enable multiple acquisitions with publicly-traded stock, borrowings on the seller's accounts receivable and using mezzanine debt – long-term, unsecured loans – and seller's notes or earn-outs, to grow rapidly. The effect on the buyer's publicly-traded common stock could be hydraulic. Thus, I knew something about venture capital, something about raising angel capital and something about leveraged buyouts, when I journeyed out on my own in 1972.

With babies coming, I had to earn more than $10,000 a year, so I departed the canyons of Wall Street and put out my own shingle, initially A. David Silver & Co. in rented space at Carl Marks & Co. where the leveraged buyout was being mass-produced. Joe Steinberg, who would go on to form Leucadia National Corp. and John W. "Jay" Jordan, who would later form The Jordan Company, one of the first great private equity funds, were there at the time, gobbling up pearls of wisdom from the late Robert G. Davidoff, one of the most successful Small Business

Investment Company managers in history. My most successful entrepreneurial client in the 1970s was ActMedia, which places mini-billboards on supermarket shopping carts, for which I raised $1,500,000 from Allstate Venture Fund, Bank America Capital and others. ActMedia was purchased by News Corporation for $650,000,000 in 1996, another great payday for me, as all of my equity raise investment banking agreements include equity as well as cash fees. I held stock in ActMedia that would grow to become worth more than $1 million dollars, and better than that, I made a dozen friends for life. Winners have so many fathers, while losers are orphans, someone once said.

After moving to Santa Fe in 1981, I changed the name of my investment bank to Santa Fe Capital Group and to become a "destination" for entrepreneurs, I began writing books on the entrepreneurial process. My 33 books have been read by hundreds of thousands of entrepreneurs and are textbooks at numerous business schools throughout the world. The side effect of writing so many books have been speaking and consulting engagements in South Africa, Malaysia, Singapore, Israel and in other countries, plus an invitation to speak at the White House to 350 women entrepreneurs based on my 1996 book, "Enterprising Women," for which I wrote short biographies on America's 100 greatest women entrepreneurs.

Since 1972 I have raised a lot of capital for a lot of entrepreneurs, and I believe I have helped to created more than 2,000,000 jobs and solved problems for sick people who needed drugs delivered to their homes, people with dengue fever, children with strep throat, farmers who until now in the age of drones did not know how much pesticide, fertilizer and water they needed for each acre and precise accounting of paychecks so that workers could be paid the right amount of money and on time.

How I measure job creation is with the help of Hoover's, which records that information. For example, Frontier Communications came to my firm for its start-up capita – that's more than 10,000 jobs. As did Amtech Corp., who you may know as founder of the E-Z Pass, which is owned by two separate companies now, each having about 10,000 employees.

Peachtree Software, developer of software for personal computers, which was acquired by ADP. ActMedia, an in-store marketing company requires a large number of people to change the signs, clean the frames and straighten them every week. Bruce Failing, Jr., and his family, conceived the idea for ActMedia, which is of a type of start-up known as the "double sale," which means the stores had to be persuaded to permit their shopping carts to be used, and the advertising agencies had to be persuaded to try a new media to attract eyeballs to their brands. I went on a number of sales calls to the stores with Bruce, and I can say without equivocation, that asking supermarket owners to change their habits is not easy. But, we did it, and now Bruce runs a venture capital fund in Darien, CT called Alerion Partners, LP. He and his staff like to consider interesting consumer-oriented deals with strong entrepreneurs at the steering wheels. I have taken a client or two to Alerion and they are growing one that I raised a round of angel capital for by the name of DeliverCareRX, Chicago, IL. It provides direct mail pharmaceutical services to older people on Medicaid and Medicare, thus saving them the time and inconvenience of taking multiple busses to their clinics or pharmacies once a month for their pills.

Another past client of mine, Robin D. Richards, a five-pete entrepreneur, and hands down Southern California's most successful entrepreneur – e.g., Lexi International, Tickets.com, MP3 Communications, Notification Technologies, Inc., and Internships.com came to me to raise Lexi's capital. He sold the last four of his start-ups for more than nine figures each. I seek Robin's counsel when I have a complex entrepreneurial opportunity in front of me. Another business genius from Southern California, Lin Wu Lan, the founder of Pacific Pioneer Insurance Co., is my favorite female entrepreneur, and by far the grittiest and most determined, and she has built a 350-person firm with her brains and fortitude.

In the last two years I have raised capital for, *inter alia,* Orion Systems Integrators, Inc., (www.orioninc.com), Princeton Junction, NJ, a software solutions provider founded by Sunil Mehta with numerous software solutions teams working around the world so that software jobs can be completed by more rapidly by moving work into different time zones;

NanoCrystals Technology, Inc., Medford, NY, founded and managed by Rameshwar N. Bhargava, PhD., and affiliated with Albert Einstein Hospital, which has developed a magnetic nanoparticles technology that can blast cancer out of the body with tiny magnets; Sol Pass, Inc. founded and managed by John Napoli (www.sol-pass.com), Denver, CO, which has developed and is selling to governments and to industry a solution to the Edward Snowden-type cyber-attack; UpDateZen, Inc., New York, NY, founded and headed up by Joreda Topi, a young lady born in Albania, raised in Germany, and now living in New York City, which is selling a mobile app that enables CEOs and CMOs to get all of their teams on the same page and reporting upwards and daily in 240 words or less on the mobile app; DJ Bennett, Inc., Washington, DC, a rapidly-growing online sports apparel retail store founded and run by Dawn J. Bennett; Canton Classic Guitars, Abiquiu, NM, a leading maker of jazz fusion guitars, founded and run by Rick Canton, now with expansion capital, sporting a new Web site, www.canonbarberguitars.com; and angel capital for Aker, a Minneapolis, MN precision farming company deploying software-laden drones for large Midwestern farms.

I have worked with and observed the minds of some legendary entrepreneurs – the late Frank Lautenberg, the late Henry Singleton, Harold Geneen, Philippe G. E. Woog (inventor of Broxodent, the first electric toothbrush), the aforementioned Bruce Falling, Lin Wu Lan and Robin Richards.

And when I see what a wonderful and useful social network that my client Kristen R. Felder built with CollisionHub.com, I smile all over myself. Kristen came to me a few years ago and said, "David, there is so much anger in the automobile collision business. The auto parts suppliers cheat the auto body shops. They over charge the client with the wrecked car. And, the auto insurers offer less money than they're supposed to. I want to start a social network where members of all of these groups can come together and talk about barbecues, and golf games, and dogs and hunting. And, through that, maybe friendships will evolve and anger will diffuse." And it happened that way. See www.collisionhub.com, funded by pleasant advertising. Kristen and I raised the launch capital from the Arkansas Angel Club.

Other social networks that I have advised and raised capital for include iboats.com, where boaters trade used boating appliances, buy new ones and discuss where to fish on the Tennessee River near Chattanooga in August; mothering.com for new mothers who want to use midwives and doulas and cloth rather than plastic; catalog.com which builds and manages social networks for others such as IBM, IKEA, Marlboro cigarettes and many more; and dealcurrent.com, which enables newspapers to compete with Groupon in offering the deal of the day. Winners all. But, I occasionally lose my mind and back a loser. It happens. I get overly-optimistic and ask my angels and my friends to send their checks and wire transfers to an entrepreneur who I did not investigate sufficiently and our stock becomes worthless. And, the good news is that backers of entrepreneurs such as myself don't learn very much from our winners. The learning comes from the deals we lose money on.

Since my background in investment banking crosses so many decades, from pre-electronic calculator, computer, internet and DNA, I have a very broad vision. For example, I see the electric washer dryer as one of the greatest inventions of all time as it freed up women to do something valuable with their time; but, it is rarely listed when Silicon Valley venture capitalists are asked to name the greatest inventions of recent times.

I traveled the country with the late Tommy J. Davis, founder of the Mayfield Fund, to raise his first $6,000,000 venture capital fund. Tommy was an early investor in Intel Corp. and over many glasses of cheap wine at Holiday Inns, from Jacksonville, FL to Jackson, MS, I learned at the knee of one of the legendary founders of Silicon Valley how to assess technology startup. I think Tommy named it and he surely named the three legs of the stool that make Silicon Valley so successful: a great university, a successful tech company spitting out entrepreneurs with tech backgrounds – he meant Hewlett-Packard – and sources of capital, in this case the early venture capital funds, Hambrecht & Quist, Mayfield Fund, Sequoia and Kleiner Perkins Caulfield and Byers.

With mentors like Tommy David and Robert Davidoff, I learned the fundamentals of judging entrepreneurs, their business models and what pieces were missing that I could help add. I will transport and disseminate to you what I learned from my tutors so that you will have herein one pocket-sized bible of fund-raising, all the steps needed from sketching out your new company's kitchen table worksheet to planning the launch to the best places to go for upfront financing.

There are 56,000,000 of you out there at the moment, like Auguste Rodin, the great French sculptor, adding a little clay here, taking away a little there, smoothing here, complicating there, in order to create a fluid business model that solves a societal or industrial or medical problem and one that sources of capital will flock to. The peculiar quality of greatness and a sense of the sublimity of the occasion stems from being alive at "the right time" and in control of events at a critical moment in history. The entrepreneur thrives on change and the instability of things. The infinite possibilities of the unpredictable future offer endless opportunities for spontaneous moment-to-moment improvisation and for their large, imaginative bold strokes that cause important events that change the course of history. Although strength comes to entrepreneurs from their clear, brightly-colored vision of – and passionate faith in – their views of the future and in their power to mold it, they know where they are going, by what means, and why. This strength enhances their energy and drive as it did with Winston Churchill's during the Battle of Britain when he said: "It is impossible to quell the inward excitement which comes from a prolonged balancing of terrible things."[1]

---

[1] Isaiah Berlin, Personal Impressions [New York: Viking, 1981]. _Back_

CHAPTER ONE

FINDING A PROBLEM IN SEARCH OF A SOLUTION

Paul Ruderman, a resident of Roseland, NJ discovered a problem in search of a solution when on Sunday morning, August 29, 2005, he watched the horror of Hurricane Katrina displace one-fourth of the 500,000 shocked and frightened residents of New Orleans, and cause the death of 2,000. Some of the deaths he learned over the ensuing days were due to the lack of coordination between New Orleans' 31 hospitals. Some of them had unused beds and doctors waiting for patients and some of them had no free beds and were turning away patients. Paul immediately went to work creating a solution, which he named Live Process Corp., which enables hospitals anywhere to accelerate deployment of the right people and resources to the right location; and coordinate organized responses through defined Emergency Operating Procedures ("EOPs") and Joint Commission compliant drill preparations. After hiring and putting into place experienced executives from the health care services field, Paul moved on to start other businesses.

What Paul did is pretty common: he saw an avoidable crisis occur before his eyes on television, and Paul responded immediately. Most new businesses arise from observing a problem either by watching it on television, reading about it in the newspapers and for more specific problems, digging into industry trade journals. The New York Times is the pre-eminent reporter of problems, many of them quite large. Local newspapers report regional problems and trade journals report problems particularized to the industry or sport that they cover. After accidentally picking up a commercial refrigeration trade journal, James Pak and William So, two Glendale, CA entrepreneurs, observed the need for more efficient refrigeration equipment for supermarkets and restaurants, and they formed Blue Air Refrigeration, Inc. in 2010. They observed top-down rules changes, driven by the revised rules of the Department of Energy that require supermarkets and restaurants to achieve significant reductions in energy use, driven by LED lighting, occupancy sensors, high-performance glass doors and high-efficiency motors.

Some problems are just so obvious they are screaming for an entrepreneurial solution. For example, there is no single company tracking payments by lobbyists to elected public officials and then tracking the bills that they write and attempt to get voted into law by their legislative body. Call this the "Jerry Maguire" opportunity, because his line in the eponymous movie, repeated over and over again, was "Show me the money."

A competitor to Fair Isaac Company, which publishes the "FICO" scores that determine our credit scores, is another company that arguably needs to be started in order to disrupt a monopolist, because their ways of doing things need to be spotlighted, to borrow the name of the 2016 Academy Awards' best picture. Monopolies need competitors, and they can usually be toppled because their employee base becomes lazy and slothful. FICO scores place a very high reliance on payment history (35%), balances – high ones are bad, low ones are good (30%), time one has used the cards (25%) and inquiries – usually because a lender has been approached for a new card or a consumer loan (10%), as recorded by Ginny Ferguson, National Credit Scoring Instructor for the National Association of Mortgage Brokers, 2004. There is no magic to FICO's model, and it appears ripe for disruption. One form of disruption is the flood of more than 200 new online consumer lenders and angel funds that have launched in the last few years from LendUp.com, that says it can make you a loan inside five minutes to FinTech Corp. (NASDAQ: FNTC), a publicly-held roller-upper of some of the struggling consumer loan companies to Seed Invest, which you will read about a few chapters from this one.

Peculiarly, many entrepreneurs apply for and receive ten to 12 credit cards in order to launch their companies, by borrowing $5,000 on each of them, only so see their FICO scores plunge into the low 600's for putting together a launch plan and a strong lift-off team. It seems to me that other factors could be selected algorithmically to determine a person's honesty and likeliness to repay a small loan, or a series of small loans. Graduation from certain colleges, ownership of a car, marriage to someone with a solid income and having monthly living expenses considerably lower than one's income.

A third problem that needs an entrepreneurial solution is directing charitable giving away from the fat and directing it to the lean. For example, Harvard University's endowment is more than $40 billion, while Doctors Without Borders are saving lives of innocent people in war-torn regions such as Southern Sudan and Syria, and lacks the resources to rebuild its field hospitals when the combatants blow them up. Ocean Conservancy is the leading charitable organization striving to save the oceans, which are warming at a ridiculously rapid rate, but it receives less than one percent of the contributions received by the Red Cross which spent more money placing its CEO and large trucks in front of areas of New Jersey's beaches hard hit by Hurricane Sandy. The New York Attorney General called out the Red Cross for using catastrophes to raise hundreds of millions of dollars, while spending *bupkes* to ease the suffering of people experiencing the effects of the catastrophe.

The opportunity to shake up the charitable giving market is ripe, because charitable giving to major U.S. organizations has been falling for the last several years. "Walkathons that used to work for the Make-a-Wish-Foundation and the March of Dimes no longer pull in the donors or the donations that they used to," Sandra Hijikada, Senior Vice President of Juvenile Diabetes Research Foundation, told NPR. "The American Cancer Society's Relay for Life saw a year-to-year drop of $45 million last year," reported David Hessekell, its President. The reason for these decreases is that "individual donors today are looking for more control and flexibility and the now have the technology in their hands to control their charitable giving on their terms," said Mr. Hessekell. It is less complicated to disrupt and solve pain in an industry that is levelling off, or in decline than one where most of the players are growing and happy with things as they are.

And notwithstanding my appeal in a 2009 book of mine, *"The Social Network Business Plan,"* that someone should bring me a social network for women rodeo riders to fund, it has not happened. The opportunity still exists. First, let's look at the size of the opportunity: 30,000,000 people attend 600 PRCA-sponsored rodeo events each year in the United States and Canada. Yet, the Professional Rodeo Cowboys Association does not recognize the women riders in its brand. And, www.prca.com has less than 1,000 monthly unique visitors ("MUVs"). Women rodeo riders do not have an active social network recording their winners, schedules, ratings and prize money and it could have a classified ad section where riders can trade saddle, boots, gloves, hats and trucks. This social network could have an online store bolted onto it, and could easily repay the cost of launching by selling cowboy, hats, boots, belts, buckles, shirts, trousers, scarves and other products. The home page could feature the logos of sponsors such as Ford Trucks, Holiday Inns, Red Bull and Hardees, at $150,000 per sponsorship per annum, thus repaying the $500,000 or so cost of launching www.rodeochicks.com. Other revenue channels include classified ads, having a brand sponsor the schedule of events page, having brand sponsor the prize money leaderboard, and the sale of autographed photos of the riders, and sharing the money with them. A forum for conversations between riders and fans could be the glue that keeps people coming back. Remember to always seek the "hunger" before starting a new business. I believe 30,000,000 people attending physical rodeos indicate hunger to get closer to the contestants. You could test that hypothesis on Facebook, as I will share you in a few pages from this one. I have funded a heck of a lot of start-ups in my day, and I believe rodeo chicks is more cattle than hat, if you know the expression. I dearly want to fund this start-up waiting to happen.

How to Learn if a Problem has Entrepreneurs Digging into Solutions:
The tragedy of the commons is an economic theory of a situation within a shared-resource system where individual users acting independently and rationally according to their own self-interest behave contrary to the common good of all users by depleting that resource.

The concept and name originate in an essay written in 1833 by the Victorian economist William Forster Lloyd, who used a hypothetical example of the effects of unregulated grazing on common land (then colloquially called "the commons") in Great Britain. The concept became widely-known over a century later due to an article written by the ecologist **Garrett Hardin** in 1968. In this context, **commons** is taken to mean any shared and unregulated resource such as **atmosphere**, **oceans**, rivers, **fish stocks**, or even a valley full of aspirant entrepreneurs, such as Silicon Valley.

The kinds of companies that I observe being financed by Santa Clara County, California's abundant venture capitalists lack very large problems, lack unique and non-duplicable solutions and the entrepreneurs have relatively little business experience. Plus, in my opinion they lack "moats', generally referred to as means of blocking competitors. But, by golly, they have huge amounts of capital, because that is new rage: over-funding.

Nick Bilton, the *New York Times* writer who covered Silicon Valley for many years, and recently left to seek a saner environment for his journalism, told *Vanity Fair*, "SF tech culture is focused on solving one problem: What is my mother no longer doing for me?" Getting a car on demand, finding something online, business productivity tools and connecting with people. These market opportunities are being pursued to their logical extremes.

My approach to launching a new business is designed for aspirant entrepreneurs who do not drink from the water fountains of Silicon Valley, but rather, live in Sheboygan, WI or Texarkana, TX – and my approach is far more procedural. There are many steps to take if you want to launch a new company the right way, with all of your ducks in a row, and with the right kind and amount of upfront financing. Silicon Valley venture capitalists seem hell bent to create unicorns, companies worth $1 billion or more. And, it is concerning to Mary Jo White, Chairman of the Securities and Exchange Commission, who told a Stanford University audience in August, 2016 that she is concerned with the area's investors "playing fast and loose with valuations" and inflating valuations to unicorn status, driven by "the publicity and pressure to meet the unicorn benchmark." (Wall Street Journal, 8/2/16.) Without a penny of revenues and without a business plan to bring in revenues since its founding in 2002, Quora, Inc. was recently valued at $900 million in a recent $80 million venture capital investment. Those kinds of valuations are for people in la-la land, and this book is not for them – they have their own reality – it is for you.

The first step in the process is, of course, conceiving of a problem in need of a solution and a solution to that problem. Step one: learning if others are ahead of you and if they are well-backed with loads of capital.

In the digital age there are means of learning if a problem is attracting problem solvers, and if so, whether or not they are well-funded. I am going to start giving you my due diligence tools, because it is important that more winners are launched. Failures chew up a lot of capital. Where I begin my due diligence to see if a problem is attracting too many well-funded entrepreneurs is to a little-known Web site called www.whois.sc.

ICANN is the organization that runs the World Wide Web, and it insists that anyone who wants to operate a Web site must have a domain name.

All domain names are listed in one place, and that place is www.whois.sc. If a name is for sale, you will find it on www.whois.sc. If it is not listed there, the domain name has not been purchased.

So, let's say you want to start a web site to persuade people to send their charitable dollars to places that need them a heck of a lot more than ivy league universities. First, you would Google (or search Bing or Yahoo, if you prefer) the question, "What is the size of the charitable giving market?" It is a question that is easily answered in several places: $358 billion was the amount of charitable giving in 2014. If you could come up with a solution to move ten percent of that amount to charitable organizations saving the planet, saving children from sex slavery, saving the ocean, and so forth and extracting a two percent annual fee for your efforts, you would hypothetically build an enterprise with revenues of $716 million per annum; enough to set up ten of your own multiple charities funded with $50 million each.

But, don't rush out and start raising money. Perhaps www.whois.sc indicates that it has been taken. But, in this case it has not. See Figure 1, a print-out from www.whois.sc indicating that www.charitiesthatcount.com is available.

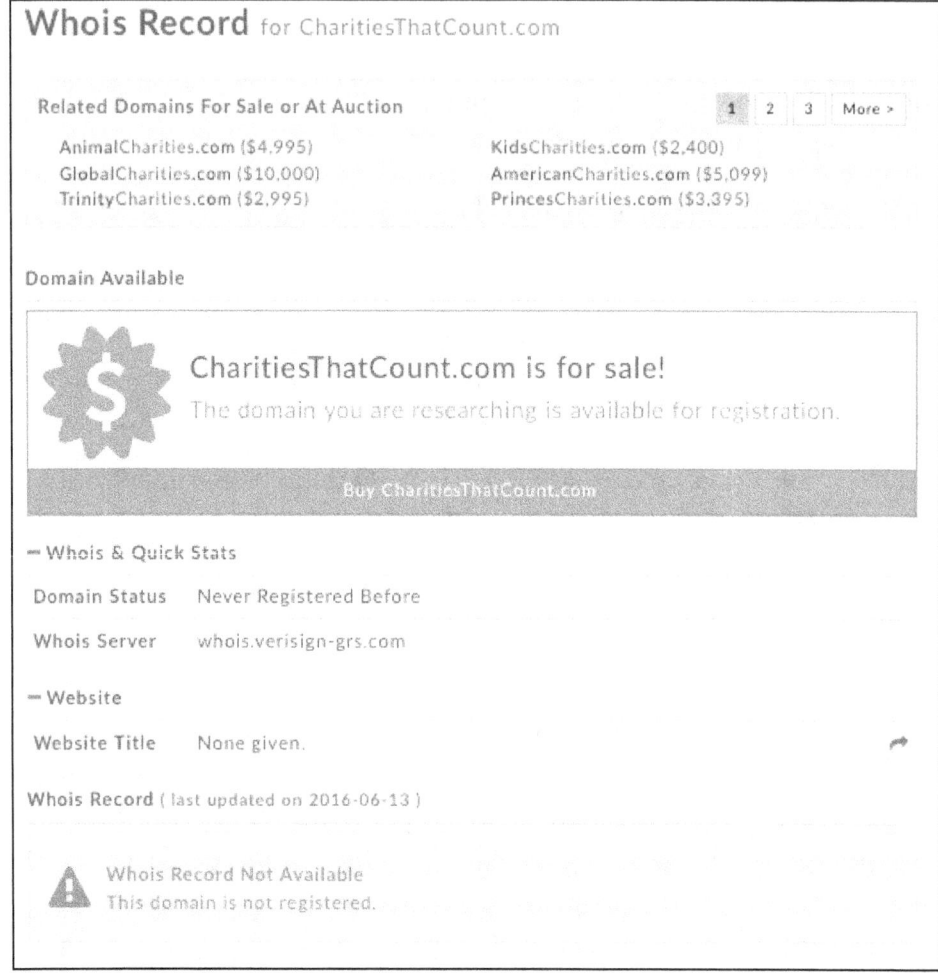

Figure 1: WHOIS.SC INDICATES WWW.CHARITIESTHATCOUNT.COM HAS NOT BEEN TAKEN

But, don't rush out and immediately start raising capital for www.charitiesthatcount.com. There is deep googling and other forms of searching to be done and an infrastructure to build. Let's see how that is done.

CHAPTER TWO

STUDYING THE PROBLEM VIA DEEP GOOGLING AND OTHER SEARCH SITES

The three words, "charities that count" is probably not the best domain name. The third word "count," may not mean the same thing to everyone. It could mean "charities that are meaningful" to you, but not to the vast multitude of members you will need to bring to your Web site and social network. And the first word in the domain name, "charities" is perhaps not as high energy a word as "giving". Better check with www.whois.sc to see if www.givingwhereitcounts.com is available. It has more action in the domain name than www.charitiesthatcount.com does. We return to www.whois.sc and we learn that www.givingwhereitcounts.com is also available.

But, we haven't dealt with the issue of "counts". That word is tricky. Let's try to replace it with the word "impact". We will type "www.givingwithimpact.com into www.whois.sc. It is also available. To block the competition, and because domain names are not very expensive -- $20.00 for one year -- you might want to buy all three. And while you are at it, remember to buy the .net and the .org versions, and if you expect to be operating in Israel, China or Chile, for instance, you will want to buy the domain names as they would appear to residents in those countries.

Who are the Pro's at the Pro-Am:
The next step in our research is to learn who are the major players in online as well as offline charitable giving. For this we go to a Web site by the name of Compete.com. This useful Web site keeps score of Monthly Unique Visitors ("MUVs") to a Web site. Your objective in scoping out Compete.com is to see if there are any big dogs in the world of disrupting the current charitable giving model, and solving pain for very needy charities, that are attempting to solve problems from starvation of people in South Sudan to enslaving children in the sex trade. In the same

way in which we sent phrases to www.whois.sc, we will do the same to Compete.com.

Let's see how this is done by typing www.charities.com into Compete.com. That search results in our viewing a Web site that is losing MUVs at a rapid rate; literally falling below the radar. The same for www.charities.org. The same for www.charitiesforchidren.org. We need to visit the actual Web sites of these organizations to learn why they may be under-performing for their members, and thereby learn something for our business model. What is happening to altruism and empathy? Is this a problem area that is overlooked top to bottom by entrepreneurs?

www.theguardian.com, an important British newspaper, reports that not only is giving on the decline, but the less well-off are giving proportionately more than the wealthy, to wit:

> "What has this got to do with charitable giving and why should we be bothered if it is falling? We have been giving since the beginning of time. We are programmed to be altruistic as well as competitive; just as the need to eat and procreate is rewarded by feeling good, the same applies to giving. Philanthropy helped us to establish the civil society we enjoy today and enabled law, education, hospitals, welfare and culture to flourish long before the industrial revolution required the state to address growing poverty. Today, perhaps because of the unprecedented material prosperity and massive debt created in the past 60 years, we are losing the plot. Just over half of us give to charities regularly but we seem to be giving less; the poor give proportionately more than the rich and only a small minority of the very rich are being philanthropic." According to John Dickson, a student of charitable giving, 10/20/13.

These are good indicators of a problem in need of a solution. But, perhaps some entrepreneurs have seen the same problem we are seeing, and have jumped into the breach with backing from a cartel of upper crust venture capital funds such as Kleiner Perkins, Sequoia, Mayfield and Accel, whose track records are the envy of the world.

We need to keep deep Googling. For the best place to see who is moving and shaking in the world of online giving, we go to LinkedIn.com and type in "Charitable Giving." LinkedIn has more than 47 million MUVs and it collects personalized statements that executives, mid-level managers and entrepreneurs say about themselves. To be kind, "it is not all bragging, but it will have to do until real bragging comes along," to paraphrase Tommy Lee Jones in the Academy Award winning movie "No Country for Old Men." On a personal note, I occupy an office in which the Coen Brothers sat with Tommy Lee, Josh Brolin and Javier Bardem when they were shooting "No County for Old Men" in New Mexico. Perhaps the karma of these amazing writers and directors from "The Big Lebowski" to "Fargo" will rub off on me and my current portfolio of start-ups.

Returning to LinkedIn, how many executives, managers and entrepreneurs talk about their charities? There are 91 executives and entrepreneurs saying wonderful things about their activities in the world of charitable giving, and we can research each organization's name that they mention. These include Planned Giving, Charitable Giving Trust, The Foundation for Charitable Giving and many more. We will need to dissect each of these to see their mission statements. The ones that have the largest number of MUVs, we will take to Crunchbase to see which venture capital funds backed them, and with how much capital. We don't want to launch a company where the competition has $50 million in their bank accounts.

The Due Diligence Process Moves to Crunchbase:
This database is a scorekeeper of which companies received start-up funding; "A" round funding, which is sometimes called "second round funding;" "B" round funding; and so forth. In addition, it tracks which venture funds or strategic funds (this refers to a venture fund owned by a business such as Intel Capital, Comcast Ventures and SalesForce Ventures) invested in the companies. The reporting is daily and if not

thorough, it directs the viewer to the Web sites of the companies that received funding the previous day.

Crunchbase is owned by TechCrunch, which AOL acquired in 2010. It provides useful data gathered in the start-up ecosystem, made up of companies, people, venture funds and events, believed to comprise around 50,000 people who submit data. Data editors at Crunchbase review the submittals to be sure of their accuracy. According to compete.com, Crunchbase has 1,318,000 MUVs in January, 2016.

An entrepreneur recently came to me with an early-stage company that was producing and selling through brick and mortar retailers a new kitchen utensil that was better than the most popular one in use for more than the last 30 years. I needed to find out if any early-stage company had recently launched with a whole lot of capital and the backing of prestigious venture capital funds. In Table I following you will see the consumer product companies that recently received funding. Note that each of them in the table plans to sell their products digitally, not through brick and mortar retail stores.

Table 1: RECENT FUNDINGS OF EARLY STAGE CONSUMER PRODUCTS COMPANIES

Allbirds	Manufactures all wool shoes, comfortable, minimizes odors, and regulates temperature; raised $2.7 million in an angel round.	3/1/16
Hungryroot	Farm fresh 7-minute meals; such as carrot noodles, cauliflower couscous, celery root noodles. $3.7 million "A" round	2/29/16
Hopscotch	Online store offering insider access to today's top baby and kids brands from around the world. $25.8 million in three rounds	2/29/16
Rocksbox	An online social network where women can rent ever-rotating designer jewelry for special events. $8.7 million in "A" round	2/26/16

The Moat, or Absence Thereof:

Although I do not know very much about these companies, in the world of online marketing, it is difficult to establish a "moat". What I mean by this, is "a deep, wide ditch surrounding a castle, fort, or town, typically filled with water and intended as a defense against attack," the dictionary definition; thus, substitute the word "newly launched company" for "castle, fort, or town" and you get my meaning. There are several things that give a moat to an early stage company, and they include strong patents, lots of capital, management team the equal of some of the greats from Jack Welch to Steve Jobs, and speed. It is frequently best to be the second company entering a new market, rather than the first. Of pioneers, it has been said, "they are people lying face down in the mud with arrows in their backs."

Crunchbase has a sister company called Deadpool which keeps records of failed companies. When I was at Kuhn, Loeb & Co., I was the fair-haired boy, having brought in Automatic Data Processing as a new client of the firm, along with Chevway Corp.; and I raised capital for a KL client by the name of Codex, the first modem manufacturer. I thought I knew a thing or two about the emerging computer revolution. So, when I advised the partners to invest in and bring their angel investors, including the Crown Agents, into Allen Babcock Computing, Inc., a computer time sharing company, I didn't know a moat from a mocking bird. Allen Babcock had more than 50 competitors, and some of them such as General Electric had much more capital and could lower price at will and take our clients. Which happened. That's how I learned about moats, and I never forgot the lesson. *You only learn from your failures in the venture capital business.* You can quote me.

Dissent as a Positive Force:

It is likely that you are starting your new company with a partner or several partners. Remember this tip from the history of Polaroid, the instant photography company. Dissent among the co-founders is very important. Groupthink is a death knell. Adam Grant describes the perils of groupthink in is majestic book, *"Originals: How Non-Conformists Move the World,":*

> "In a famous analysis, Yale psychologist Irving Janis identified groupthink as the culprit behind numerous American foreign-policy disasters, including the Bay of Pigs invasion and the Vietnam War. According to Janes, groupthink occurs when people 'are deeply involved in a cohesive in-group' and their 'strivings for unanimity override their motivation to realistically appraise alternative courses of action.'"

Dr. Herbert Land invented a system for polarizing light, which enabled not only instant photography, but also pocket calculators, sunglasses, 3-D movie glasses and the U-2 spy plane. Land amassed 535 patents, second only to Thomas Edison. Steve Jobs called him "...a national treasure."

And his business model while growing Polaroid in a decade to $900 million in sales was based on the commitment start-up model. Rather than placing reliance on star engineers and people with professionally successful resumes, Land hired a diverse group of artists, veterans and people with diverse skills who spoke of "love" and "family" in their interviews. They demonstrated intense passion for the Polaroid mission. It is this model – commitment to the mission – which James Baron, Michael Hannon and Diane Burton have proven in their study of two hundred tech start-ups from the fields of telecom, network, bio-sciences and medical devices, to produce more winners in tech start-ups, than the other two models, hiring star engineers and hiring professionals with the best resumes.

Polaroid was inventing digital photography, which of course, over-took instant photography in the 1990s, but Dr. Land believed that his key product would continue to thrive and survive even with the onslaught of digital photography. The false assumption was this: that customers would always want hard copies of photographs. The team around Dr. Land drank the same Kool-Aid as he did, and it became groupthink, and it killed the company.

When an entrepreneurial team comes to my office to describe their start-up, and if they exhibit groupthink, nodding when a partner speaks, or saying, "I agree with Jim on that point," they lose me. I like dissension, arguments, questioning hypotheses and different sets of assumptions among the co-founders. At the same time, commitment to the mission by the co-founders is very important to me.

CHAPTER THREE

MEASURING THE SIZE OF THE OPPORTUNITY

The charitable giving market has score keepers and they tell us that it is around $358 billion and declining. That is a perfect market to enter; that is, one that is large and troubled.

But, what about a more diffuse market? Women rodeo riders is a more difficult market to gauge. Google tells us that 30 million people attend a rodeo event every year. If we assume that each attendee spends $20 at a rodeo event, then the market size is $600 million. This doesn't account for the money spent by the riders and their teams on their gear, or the money spent by the event promoters on horses, bulls, calves and lambs. It is a robust market, with barely scratching the surface of the digital world.

It is absolutely vital to attempt to put a number on the size of the market that you are thinking of entering to either disrupt – if you want to, say, take down FICO, with a new means of rating peoples' credit worthiness – or you want to expand it by taking it to digital – if you want to, say, create a social network for women rodeo riders. Another business model is the "irritation" model. This model presumes that you want to irritate the industry leader by taking market share from it, so that it will acquire your company just to get rid of it.

The Irritation Business Model:

Think of markets dominated by a single brand, with near monopoly power. You can be certain that their management team and middle managers are not among the most creative people in business. They could mail their jobs in; so boring is it to have monopoly power. Some of the brands are much too powerful to knock off. Tabasco sauce is one of them. Pixar, the inventor of animated movies, irritated Walt Disney Enterprises so severely that Disney paid billions to acquire it. From a standing start in 1995 with the release of "Toy Story," which grossed $191,665,000 in U.S. box office revenues, animated movies have grown to U.S, box office revenues of $1,323,485,375 and 156,997,074 tickets sold in 2015, according to www.the-numbers.com/DigitalAnimation. And that does not include DVD sales. The late Steve Jobs' estate is in the billions of dollars primarily because he conceived of, launched, operated and built Pixar. He actually had a smaller ownership of Apple Computer Co.

One of my portfolio companies, the developer of a natural language search engine by the name of Cognition Technologies, Inc., for which I raised angel capital in 2002, was acquired by Nuance Communications, Inc., in 2013, largely because it had won a contract from Microsoft Corp. to make its search engine, Bing, able to produce the right answer to a search question each time rather than hundreds of answers as Google does. That was not our goal. We thought Lexis Nexus, a leading collector of information for the legal community, would acquire Cognition, because the information we could gather with our natural language search engine was more precise and accurate than the information that Lexis Nexus gathered from daily court records, packaged and sold. Rather, they became a customer and did not think of acquisition.

The Newsletter, Publishing Start-up Opportunity:

A little known fact: one-third of the *Forbes 400* achieved their wealth through publishing, or from their parents' publishing ventures. The late Walter Annenberg, whom you may know as Ambassador to Great Britain under President Ronald Reagan, inherited his wealth from his father's highly successful venture, the *Daily Racing Forum,* a newsletter that provided detailed information on every horse and every jockey at every racetrack hosting races on those race days. Bettors could not place their bets without reading the Annenberg's newsletter. Talk about finding the hunger and feeding it. Gambling is addictive and betting on horse races is just plain fun.

Speaking of gathering, slicing and dicing and then selling information, aspirant entrepreneurs can seize the newsletter publishing opportunity of a nascent industry by moving swiftly, stealthily and intelligently. Within hours of digital search of the type I have been describing, you will be able to see if the opportunity is still virginal. To become the next Moe

Annenberg, you must enter a new and emerging industry and have the ability through Google, Bing and Yahoo, our three wonderful search engines, to gather and publish all of the vital information in the emergent industry that you are aware of.

The late Patrick J. McGovern, who you may know as the founder and publisher of *Computerworld* magazine, built an empire named International Data Group, Inc., a publisher of 62 magazines and newspapers. McGovern spotted the opportunity in the late 1960's, at about the time of the birth of the semiconductor, which beckoned the computer revolution.

Going much deeper through the doors that the personal computer opened, let's take a look at the unique entrepreneurial brain of Sheldon Adelson, one of the world's ten richest men. You may know of Sheldon Adelson as the owner of casinos in Las Vegas and Macao, and as a backer of political candidates who are loyal supporters of Israel. But, the back story is quite fascinating. In 1972, when Adelson had lost one and a half million dollars in a Wall Street crash, he purchased *Communications User* magazine, and attended an unrelated trade show sponsored by the owner of a condominium conversion business. He learned that the trade show owner also published a magazine, and it immediately occurred to him that trade shows were "living magazines." He changed the name of his magazine to *Data Communications User,* and in 1979 as the personal computer was emerging, he launched COMDEX in Las Vegas, which grew to become the leading trade show in the computer and software industry, until Adelson sold it to a Japanese buyer for $2 billion at the top of the Internet bubble in 2000. At its peak, Adelson bought up every seat on every flight in and out of Las Vegas and every bed in every hotel during COMDEX. His company, The Interface Group, became a facilities manager of 30 other trade shows. Note that all of Adelson's trade shows published the Trade Show Daily, chocked full of stories about the trade show events and accompanied by ads. I chatted with Adelson frequently in the speakers' and press room at COMDEX, because I was a speaker or a panelist at dozens of COMDEXES. I have always used speaking at trade shows as a means of attracting entrepreneurs to my investment bank.

Does the mobile app industry have a newsletter and trade show? How about the peer-to-peer file sharing industry? I don't think so. The pioneering, but illegal, peer-to-peer file-sharing service called Napster went online in 1999; that's how old this nascent industry is, yet no trade show or newsletter. Napster provided access to millions of music tracks. Although Napster was shut down, it inspired a host of peer-to-peer services. These include Skype (for telephony), Spotify (for music streaming), bitcoin (an alternative currency) and R3 CEV, a new start-up launched by David Rutter, a long-time financial services industry manager, which is developing a trusted standard of internal ledgers for financial institutions to eliminate the need for counterparty endorsement such as notaries and title insurance. Rutter foresees a replication of the internet's facilitation of instant, global communication, with his combination of time-stamped and digitally signed transactions hosted on a globally accessible ledger, with users authenticating themselves with secret passcodes and cell phone numbers to prove they are who they are and where they should be. If Rutter pulls it off – and 25 major financial institutions are testing his model – the savings to financial institutions, borrowers and home and building buyers, could be in excess of $20 billion a year, according to an official at Bank Santander.

There are spin-offs to the newsletter publishing business. Adelson segued into the world's biggest trade show in terms of attendees – more than 110,000 a year at its peak – as well as into facilities management of trade shows owned by others. The trade show business is extraordinarily cash flow positive. At its core, it is the rental of hotel conference rooms for a flat fee and then renting space to exhibitors for three or four days; plus, publishing a daily trade show daily newspaper, selling sponsorship banners, permitting brands to sponsor coffee cups, notepads and shopping bags, and selling tchochkies of the event from hats to T-shirts and from pencils to visors.

And there is the virtual trade show. The newsletter publisher of the nascent peer-to-peer file sharing service doesn't need to rent hotel conference room space, he or she can produce the trade show virtually. Members only, of course, and membership has its price. Booth space can be virtual with the brands' creating avatars to man the booths and attendees purchasing avatars at the entrance to visit the booths, and attend speeches and seminars. The digital age has permitted virtual trade shows, and the use of avatars, which McKinsey & Co. and others call *transformational* events. By using an avatar, we (you or me, or your sales person at the virtual trade show) are represented in the media, and it fundamentally changes how we interact and transact business with others, who are also using avatars.

First of all, it is a fun experience, because we have to dress our avatars, which is like being a child all over again. Stanford University professors tested the heart rate of people deploying avatars, and it was faster by 10 heart beats a minute than for people playing a game as themselves. People are more outspoken when they are deploying an avatar, and the avatar is more outspoken in responding. Thus, feedback is more instantaneous and more direct. The objective of trade shows is for the attendees to learn what is new and different, and for exhibitors to meet as many potential customers as they can. Both sides believe they will come away with success. Therapists call that self-efficacy. The essence of self-efficacy is belief in the source of one's destiny. Those people with high self-efficacy believe that they control situations rather than the reverse. It can be achieved by watching as well as by doing. The trade show, virtual or real, provides a broad panoply of one's industry, with all the players, avatars controlled by players or the players themselves, and it will never go away. It is vital to every industry from ophthalmology to consumer packaged goods. And to own the leading newsletter and the leading trade show of a nascent industry that you believe is going to grow into tens of thousands of participants, could be the business you launch and operate.

The Private Facebook Business Opportunity:

Jay Z, one of the more talented entrepreneurs of our day, circulated a business plan that happily arrived at my door by the name of Jay Z's ESN, which stands for "enterprise social network." It is no secret that Facebook is the dominant social network; that it has 1.4 billion members, whom it encourages to give more and more information about their "likes," so Facebook can rent their names to marketing companies who want to send their messages to certain demographic groups with specific likes. Facebook is a profiler, and it does what it does so brilliantly, that its market capitalization is $326.2 billion. Exxon Mobil's is $310 billion and Microsoft's is $425 billion, to bring things into perspective.

Facebook encourages its members to increase their number of "likes." This captures our tribal behavior; i.e., to gain more likes than others have. To do this, we tell more about ourselves. This enables advertisers who rent the use of Facebook members to shoot their pitches to just the right demographic. Variable rewards to the advertisers drive repeat action.

Getting back to Jay Z, who seeks to create a private version of Facebook, by bringing lots of celebrities to an enterprise social network that he has created. He has the clout and power to bring celebrities and their fans to his enterprise social network; for instance, Beyoncé with her 106 million likes, Rihanna with her 90 million, Taylor Swift with her 73 million and so forth. His argument is that celebrities and companies, such as Red Bull with 43 million Facebook likes use Facebook for their online fan and customer care, and in so doing effectively outsource their shareholder value to Facebook.

Facebook makes money four ways on these celebrities and celebrity-like companies including from ads presented to its members, from insights generated by members' social interactions on Facebook, from direct messages sent to members of Facebook and from revenues from off brand (or competing) messages sent to members. Jay Z points out that enterprise social networks with his celebrities and celebrity brands can hold conversations with fans and customers, and the brands and the celebrities and the fans can do a considerable amount of messaging, and those messages begin to define the demographic that brands and corporations will pay to advertise to. In that way, revenues are pulled away from Facebook and pushed into Jay Z's enterprise social network. The gains for advertisers is that competition in the profiling business will force Facebook to either offer more services or lower price. The gains for customers is that they will gain control over who sells their conversations, and perhaps they will be able to negotiate a share of the sale price. And the gain for the founders of enterprise social networks is they can make money the Facebook way, with modifications that set them apart.

Think of all the enterprise social networks that can be created, to bring back some of the shareholder value that has been transferred to Facebook. They include all of the team sports, all of the solo sports such as fishing, boating, golf, tennis, archery and running. Sports apparel manufacturers would love the concept. Then, there could be ESN's for college students, coin and stamp collectors, chefs, investors and the list goes on.

CHAPTER FOUR

WILL YOUR NEW BUSINESS IDEA SUCCEED?

The great African- American comedian, Stepin' Fetchit, would famously tell Moms Mabley, "First I'm gonna tell you what I'm gonna tell you, 'n then I'm gonna tell you what I told you." That is an important opening statement to my time tested formula for predicting the success of new businesses. It isn't perfect, but few things are. But, as the magnificent actress of the 40's Alexis Smith belted out in the Stephen Sondheim musical "Follies," I'm still here. I am in my 44th year of backing entrepreneurs, and I must have produced more winners than losers because I'm still here. And, here is the formula that I have relied on for most of those years:

$V = P \times S \times E$

Where V = Valuation or the wealth eventually created by the business;

> P = The size of the Problem (or Opportunity if you prefer);
> S = The elegance of the Solution; and
> E = The quality of the Entrepreneurial team.

I give the number 3 to very high ratings for P, S and E. For example, we know as a fact that in Saudi Arabia, which has a population of 28,705,000 (according my *Economist* diary), 29 percent of the people have Type 1 or Type 2 diabetes. The percentage is growing by one or two percent per annum. As it is a fairly wealthy country, many people do not exercise because it is considered a sign of not being well-to-do. Worse than that, the American diet of Frito's and Pepsi Cola has caught on, and the combination of slothfulness and a sugary diet is driving diabetes in the Saudi Kingdom.

Would the government pay $5,000 a year to purchase insulin and provide medical care for the Kingdom's 8,300,000 diabetics? If so, the entrepreneur who addresses this problem is looking at one worth $41.5 billion and growing. That is what I call a "Big P" opportunity and they are most often found in life sciences and health care.

For lesser P opportunities, ask yourself, "How many people are hungry for this solution that I'm thinking about or I have conceived?" And, multiply that number by the price of the S, the solution. In the digital age, the S – the solution – is frequently paid for by a third party. For instance in the social network, www.patientslikeme.org, the conversations of members who discuss their ailments with other members, the conversations are sold to big pharmaceutical companies and the National Institutes of Health. The same is true at www.sermo.com, a social network in which physicians discuss treatments, insurance issues and new drugs and diagnostic techniques (56,432 MUVs in January, 2016 according to Compete.com), the conversations of the physicians are sold to the same buyers, and a portion of the revenues is shared with the physicians.

An elegant solution is one with a patent, or a moat that protects the company from being attacked by competitors with much more capital and an ability to capture customers more rapidly. Speed to market is important: note how Uber jumped right into the market of getting a much needed taxi quickly – not patent in the uberization of the taxi market, merely knowing how to use GPS and knowing how to create a mobile app.

How is the quality of the E factor – the Entrepreneurial team measured? As the greatest thinker and write on the subject of management, the late Peter H. Drucker wrote: "Managers must know how to do the right thing. They can hire people to do the things right." When you launch your new company, you may be hiring people for the first time. You may have to make these decisions on the fly or while multi-tasking. What I like to see in an entrepreneur who is going to be a manager for the first time is that she creates a Board of Advisors. This board should be composed of wise people from industry who can provide guidance concerning hiring people to do things right.

The purpose of being in business in the first place is to make your product or service a substitute for all other competitive products or services and to make their products or services no substitute for yours.

To achieve that, your new company must also have at least six out of the eight DEJ Factors. DEJ stands for "demonstrable economic justification." If your new company has high scores in the V=PxSxE equation (no zeroes, because zero times any integer equals zero, and that means V becomes zero) and if it contains eight out of the eight DEJ Factors, then you will require very little capital to launch your new business and it will have a very high probability of success. But, if it contains only six of the eight DEJ Factors, it will require tens of millions of dollars, and even hundreds of millions of dollars to succeed. Following are the eight DEJ Factors with short explanations:

1. *Existence of a large number of receivers:* Are there many potential consumers of your solution, and are they aware of the problem that your solution addresses? You can imagine that educating people about a problem that they aren't aware that they have is quite expensive. In the digital age, you can Google (the new word for "search") for phrases that people use to describe what might be irritating them. And, once you find those search phrases, you can convert them into messages and for relatively few dollars rent the names of Facebook members who have also discussed those issues, and "bingo!" you have found a large number of receivers for the solution you intend to pass along to them. Never before in the history of commerce, and thanks to Mark Zuckerburg, the founder of Facebook, and Steve Jobs, the founder of the smartphone, have entrepreneurs and the brands been able to send messages and ads with a rifle shot to people who seek that specific solution, via their smartphones, often when they are near the place where the solution is marketed. And for the latter, thank you GPS.

Nir Eyal, in his book *"Hooked,"* cites a factor which is also key to growing the Demand curve so that it meets your Supply curve rapidly and without hiccups and distractions. The factor is "Virtual Cycle Time," which is the amount of time it takes a user to invite another user to join a social network. If it takes only one day, a social network can grow into the millions of members very quickly. User engagement at a rapid rate is key to growing demand.

2.   *Homogeneity of receivers:* Will the consumers of your solution accept a standard product or service, or will you have to customize it? In the field of business to business marketing, with business productivity solutions for instance, many entrepreneurial companies have to provide a basic suite of services and add bells and whistles to create a premium service. At my investment bank, we work with quite a few managed service providers. These are reincarnations of H. Ross Perot's facilities management systems company, EDS. They literally take a client's information technology facility into their shop and send work up to the cloud where clients and customers can access it, with proper security codes. And the managed service providers remove obsolete and redundant operations, saving the clients quite a bit of money. There is some customizing, but the profit margins are worth the effort. That is known as a high "CLTV" or customer lifetime value. That is the amount of money made from a customer before he or she switches to a competitor. When a managed service provider locks onto a SMB, small or medium-size business, it typically holds onto that client for many years. Other companies with high CLTV numbers are credit card and auto insurance companies. You can tell high CLTV vendors because they spend so much on advertising. We have come to love or laugh with GEICO's gecko and Flo of Progressive; they are ubiquitous, like your spouse's hubristic cousins.

3.   *Existence of Qualified Receivers:* You are pleased with the Supply side of your business. You have invented a gizmo that will inform people with second homes in the country or at the beach, when there is a leak in their roofs and in times of heavy rains, their ceilings are accumulating water. A sensor on the ceilings of several of the rooms can send a message to the customers' cell phone when that occurs. How do you persuade the Demand side of your business model that this is a problem the customers should worry about? It is difficult. If you ask members of the home insurance industry to lower their rates for customers who pay you $10.00 a month for your solution, you may get a series of "No, thank you's," or "Let's run a pilot with one hundred of our clients to see how

many leaks actually occur." Neither response is what you were hoping to hear. My advice: don't start a company in which you need to persuade potential customers that they have a problem. There are so many problems in the world; no need to invent new ones.

4.   *Existence of Competent Providers:* Will the solution delivery method require a lot of expensive feet-on-the-street salespeople, and will there be a long cycle from first presentation to sale. The latter is known as contact to contract. If it is long, it will eat up working capital like a hungry lion. However, if your solution is marketed through a social network, you will want to meet Dmitri Williams, founder and CEO of Ninja Metrics. Williams holds a patent jointly with the University of Southern California, that finds the influencers in social networks. Many of Ninja Metrics' sales have been to game companies that seek to encourage dwarfs to buy suits of armor to enable them to defeat the zombies and win the love of the princess; but, Williams has modified the influencer algorithms to be useful to social networks. And the more an online service uses an algorithm, the stronger the algorithm that drives traffic and purchases becomes.

5.   *Absence of Institutional Barriers to Entry:* Is there a restriction that must be removed in order to access the public? An example would be having to clear a therapy for a serious disease with the United States Food and Drug Administration ("FDA"). They are the cop on the beat in world of life sciences start-ups and one of the reasons that American life sciences companies often launch their new products in Europe where the barrier to entry is less costly. One on my firm's clients, NanoTheranostics, Inc., Medford, NY, ("NANO")has developed solutions in the diagnostic field and in the therapy field for cancer. It uses magnetic nano particles to light up the tumor and to hold the chemotherapy on the tumor, while a magnet outside the body blasts the tumor. It has achieved great success with mice, but to apply for the right to test its therapy on humans, NANO must apply for an Initial New Drug ("IND") application, which is a multi-million-dollar procedure and one that takes around two years. Thus, the diagnostic product, one that enables physicians to see the disease more

clearly will be pushed first, because it is superior to the current method of "lighting up" the disease area. And achieving regulatory approval for a diagnostic is much less expensive than for a therapy.

6. *The 'Hey it Really Works' Factor:* If your product or service requires a lot of advertising dollars to achieve market share, the first solution that should pop into your mind is, "Can I find customers on Facebook?" If you visit the Flat Iron District of New York City, a region bounded on the South by 14th Street and on the North by the old garment district, say 39th Street, on the East by Broadway and on the West by the Hudson River, you will see that 800+ mainly social network companies received $7.7 billion of angel or venture capital in 2015. That is a stunning number. Why the Flat Iron District? Because that is where Google and Facebook placed their East Coast operations, and where digital advertising agencies and social network companies deposit billions of their dollars into the Google and Facebook mail slots. When you search for the phrases that people use on Google, then convert those phrases to messages that you send to the members of Facebook who say they would like to see a new deodorant or a jalapeno flavored tomato sauce or a mobile app that organizes their projects more efficiently, then you have cut right through the "Hey, it really works" factor. Unilever did exactly this and created a line of hygiene products called Dove for Men, and added close to a billion dollars of brand new revenues to Unilever, by combining search with the help of Google Ad Works to having Facebook serve up the email addresses of men who mentioned something about smelling, showering or feeling more refreshed.

7. *Invisibility:* Can your new company be built stone by stone with stealth, very quietly and without press releases and announcements? Will your personality permit operating invisibly while you take market share from an established monolithic monopolist? Remove your name from LinkedIn and inform your fellow managers to do the same. The late Henry Singleton, founder of Teledyne (the pulsating shower head is one of its products), made 130 acquisitions and build Teledyne into a company worth$3.1 billion over a period of ten years, while operating form a grey,

metal desk reclaimed at an auction of old Navy furniture, and one assistant, Themos Miklos, with whom I remain friendly. Called the "Sphinx" because he would never talk to the press, Singleton was named by Warren Buffett, the best manager in the U.S.

At my first job in the late 1960's at Chase Manhattan Bank, we provided loans to Malcom P. McLean, founder of the container-shipping industry with his company, Seal-Land Services, Inc., Port Elizabeth, NJ, to enable him to purchase moth-balled ships from World War II and put "honeycombs" into their hulls to hold truck containers. He operated stealthily, making the purchases through different agents so as not to have the old ships suddenly rise in price. As a side note, the idea to invent the container shipping industry came to McLean from someone who said the dockworkers at the Brooklyn Navy Yards were cutting holes into barrels of scotch being shipped to America from Europe to the dismay of liquor distributors who were paying scotch that they were not getting.

8.   *Optimum Cost Price Relationship:* The higher the gross profit margin, the more successful the business will be, because you will have more cash to use for marketing and to reward employees. With software companies, the cost of goods sold are quite low, and the gross profit margin very high, usually around ninety-five percent. Most venture capitalists prefer No COGS businesses, which is the case with social media and social network companies. The downside of Silicon Valley funding so many social network companies is a decline in productivity, which is measured by the Gross Domestic Product, or "GDP." Productivity goes down when more and more people work from home, because it results in fewer car trips, fewer purchases of gasoline, a decline a need for shoes and business attire, and smaller dry-cleaning bills. Then, the smart phone has cut into sales of alarm clocks, document scanners, maps, kitchen timers and flashlights, all of which exist on smart phones. People are more productive but that is not reflected in GDP. Source: Ernest Battifarano, New York *Times*, B8,

Meet Float and Moat: The maximum achievable score is a 45 that I would give any start-up would be 45 points. Here is how you could get there. First, if the values you assign to P, S and E are each a three, then you know that 3 x 3 x 3 = 27. Then, the Eight DEJ factors are worth one point apiece, or eight total. If you have all eight, then you are at 35. The next six points have to do with float and moat. Float means the customer pays you in advance, before you deliver a product. I give float a value of three. Moat means your protection from competition. It is a deep, wide body of water that surrounds a caste or other fortification. If your business is set up in a manner that the competition cannot detect what you are doing, or if you have strong patents, or if you move stealthily and quietly, that could be your moat. If your start-up has float and moat, give yourself six more points, and you are at 41.

Digital Marketing: The final four points are yours if you can bring customers to your social network or to your Web site using digital marketing. This is critical, because digital marketing is much less expensive than all other forms of marketing. What is it, you ask? It is a two-step process. The first step of which is to pay Google Ad Words to find all of the search terms and phrases that people use when they are searching the problem area for which your start-up is building a solution. Let's say you want to start a business that takes young archeologists to ruin sites where they can dig for old artifacts and Australopithecus bones, paid for by university endowment funds who get to keep the finds. You need to find the "hunger" and who has it, and how do they express it. Let's say Google Ad Words finds these most-used phrases: "I want to go on digs." "How can I go on artifact digs?" "Who organizes digs for artifacts?" "Joining a dig in Africa." The most frequently used word was "digs," and thus, the message to find young archeologists should incorporate the word digs.

The next step is to create the message, and this can be done with the help of a digital advertising shop like VaynerMedia, in New York City, arguably the best of its kind. The message is shaped to appeal to young people, let's say age 15 to 22, who have mentioned on Facebook their love of archeology, or their desire to go on a dig or needing to build their resume for an archeological job by having actual dig experience.

Facebook makes its revenues by encouraging people to talk about themselves, then profiling them and then renting their names to marketers or early-stage companies that wish to capture them as members of their community and customers for their product or service. Facebook does not charge very much for the names they rent -- $4.00 per thousand. And, the response rate can be as high as five or six percent. Thus, if your budget can spring for $4,000 you can send a message to 1,000,000 "junior archeologists" on Facebook and capture perhaps 50,000 to begin your business. That is why I award four points to this last attribute of a start-up. If you can find 50,000 customers to start your business as inexpensively and as smoothly as the Google-to-Facebook-to-your-cash-register, then I would love to see it. But, for now, this is an amazing and inexpensive way to achieve upfront financing from upfront payments of customers found on Facebook. In the digital age, start-ups do not need as money as they did years ago. Digital marketing is so much less expensive than putting a sales force on the street.

Special Note to Women Entrepreneurs: I have found through my years of making and losing money on start-ups that the higher the number of points an entrepreneur objectively believes his business has, using the Silver Scoring Method above, the less start-up capital is needed to achieve a successful launch. By that I mean, make the cash register ring with deposits that exceed all expenses, and make the cash register ring with more deposits each month that follows. For example, if a start-up objectively possesses 45 points, it can lift-off with a few hundred thousand dollars. Remember, one of the big important values is upfront financing from customers.

No single group of entrepreneurs knows the singularity of importance of having customers pay for a product or service before the product or service is delivered than do women entrepreneurs. They have historically had difficulties in raising capital from venture capitalists for a variety of reasons, as I describe in my book *"Enterprising Women: Lessons from Our*

100 of the Greatest Entrepreneurs of Our Day," AMA, 1992. Because of this book, I was invited to be a guest speaker to 350 women entrepreneurs assembled at the White House by the staff of President Bill Clinton. I had the honor of being seated at lunch with the late Anita Roddick, founder of the Body Shop chain, Lillian Vernon, founder of a catalog retailer of the same name, Mary Kay Ash, founder of the multi-level marketing company of the same name and several aspiring women entrepreneurs. The topic was their difficulties in raising capital.

Lillian Menasche, who changed her name to her company's name taken from her hometown of Mt. Vernon, NY, began placing ads for personalized purses and boots in *Seventeen* magazine in 1951, at the age of twenty-four. This may not strike you has having a differentiator, but the personalizing of a product makes it virtually non-returnable. People simply don't or feel they can't return a purse or a pair of boots with their name on them. So, stroke of brilliance, Ms. Vernon, as all other catalogs of the day had not thought of personalization. The Federal Trade Commission sets sixty days as the outside limit for sending a customer the things he or she ordered and prepaid for. Ms. Vernon had a spread between the money she received for the products she advertised and the cost of the products themselves, and the spread was not only her profit but her working capital. Eventually, the success of Lillian Vernon Co. grew to a 120-page catalog featuring 750 items, which she launched in 1956. When Ms. Vernon retired, and her sons didn't want the business, she sold it to Regent Companies, a California private equity fund. Among the many models that Ms. Vernon hired to display her goods was Marla Maples, the second wife of Donald Trump.

Jean Nidetch, born to a cab driver father and a manicurist mother, did not have financial backing to go to college, but she took a business course and went to work in various secretarial jobs. However, she was a severe over-eater, and searched high and low for a means to force her to stop eating and lose weight. In 1963, she formed Weight Watchers International, Inc. Its business model was quite simple: Jean said, "I am going to ask overweight women, and men, to come to a hotel conference room one night a week, and pay me two dollars for the privilege of standing up and telling the crowd what has caused them to get fat and what they intend to do about it." It was group therapy writ large. The group helped everyone fight over-eating. Ms. Nidetch learned the art of making money with the seminar business model: wide aisles, lots of breaks and a table in the back room where she sold books, Weight Watchers scorecards (for measuring pounds dropped each week), aprons, caps, recipe books, and more. H.J. Heinz bought the company in 1978 for moderate eight figures.

But, women have it tough when it comes to seeking launch capital from venture capitalists. In the chapters that follow I will dwell on the types of upfront financing that do not require pitching business plans to male MBA graduates who have no operating experience and who are afraid of strong women. There are many ways to launch a company without raising angel capital, and women entrepreneurs need to know how the game is played. But, what ho! There are women-owned funding sources, and I will describe several of them. Natalia Oberti Noguera, 32, founded Pipeline Angels in 2011 when only 12.0% of angel investors were women and only 4.0% were minorities according to the Center of Venture Research at the University of New Hampshire. Pipeline invests in women-owned social ventures and Ms. Oberti Noguera pulls the capital from a group of fifty women, many of whom she found by noticing their charitable giving activities and approaching them. Born and raised in Central America, Ms. Oberti Noguera completed two master's degrees and in 2008 launched New York Women Social Entrepreneurs, a group formed to support "the next generation of women change-makers." As she built the community from six to 200 members, she told the FT, "Whenever these women who had super-interesting disruptive business models were sharing their ideas, people were excited and asked where they could donate." But, the same investors balked when it was revealed to them these were for-profit ventures. The double standard shocked her, and she said, "If a woman is saying she's going to change the world, the assumption is she's launching a non-profit. People don't assume the same for a man." This oxymoron led her to begin Pipeline, where a woman whose business model is bent on disrupting a problem or hurt suffered by many and introducing a solution that pleases all can achieve capital, support and business advice.

CHAPTER FIVE

PROVIDING ANSWERS TO THE FIVE MAIN QUESTIONS SMART INVESTORS ASK

When approaching a smart investor, or a group of investors who are not skilled in judging the likely outcome of a start-up company, but have a financial advisor, there are five questions that the entrepreneur must answer in a satisfactory manner. These are the following:

1. How much can I make?
2. How much can I lose?
3. How do I get my money out?
4. Who says this deal is any good?
5. Who else is in this deal?

It is in the best interests of the entrepreneur and the investor that either a fast "no" or a long "yes" is achieved, rather than a fast "yes" without due diligence or a long "no," which is a heart breaker. Accordingly, these five points should be covered in the first few pages of the entrepreneur's pitch book. It is sometimes referred to as the Investor Deck, the "PPM," which means the Private Placement Memorandum, the "CIM," which means the Confidential Information Memorandum or the Offering Circular.

When I raise capital for a start-up or early-stage entrepreneurial venture, I like to submit a one-pager which tells the story, answers the five questions, but disguises the company's name. This one-pager is called a "Teaser," and its task is several. First, its primary task is to generate sufficient interest that the recipient requests the CIM, PPM, Offering Circular or Investor Deck. (I am going to go with "Investor Deck" for simplicity.) Its secondary task is when the Investor Deck is requested, I can examine the portfolio of the venture capital fund that requested it to see if they are on a "fishing expedition". What that means is the venture capital fund has a similar company in its portfolio that it has already funded and wants to see comparable business models, and perhaps copy my client's. Non-disclosure agreements are typically gainsayed by venture capital funds, so it is best to be wary in dealing with them. With virtually every other source of capital except equity investors, non-disclosure agreements are used, and I strongly urge you to have the recipient party sign a non-disclosure agreement, also referred to as an "NDA" before you send it your business plan.

The third point I want to make concerning the reason for sending a no-name teaser to potential equity investors is that you never want to send a long memorandum to someone you don't know. It is a bit of an insult. And it will not be read, unless a trusted friend of the equity investor introduced you. A stranger must always send a teaser, and it should be no more than one page in length. Obviously, it should end with how you can be reached.

My experience raising capital for EarthLink, Inc. in 1994 provides answers to the five big questions, particularly the validators: "Who else is in the deal?" The very young founder of EarthLink, Sky Dayton, brought in some well-known names for his seed round, thus ordaining him with respectability.

I met Bob Kavner in 1981 when I moved to New Mexico. He was an accountant with Coopers & Lybrand. We talked for a while about our mutual love – entrepreneurship – and then I lost track of him for several years. Then he surfaced, and not timidly, but like a sizzling rocket. He was a member of the audit team, which worked on AT&T, and, after a few years, AT&T brought him onboard as Chief Financial Officer. Bob moved up the ladder to Chief Operating Officer and in 1994, he was lured away to become CEO of NCR, the old cash register maker, which needed a fixer-up.

Not to get too far ahead of the story, but in 1996, when Xing Technology Corp., of San Luis Obispo, asked me to raise a round of venture capital, I asked Bob to invest and join as Chairman to provide advice. The late Howard Gordon had discovered a means of sending music and video over the Internet, known today as MP3 ("Motion Picture 3") and we needed to license the use to Internet Service Providers. The quite brilliant Ron Burkle blessed us with a $4 million investment, and we were off to the races. Real Networks, Inc. acquired Xing for nine figures, and it was a great payday for all of us who were involved at the beginning.

Getting back to 1994, perhaps it was a desire to become the top CEO of a digital company, but after improving NCR's business model, Bob segued over to Overture, a search engine company that Yahoo acquired for a billion dollars, thus giving Yahoo search capability. At about that time, Bob asked me to help out a fascinating young man launch EarthLink, which Bob had invested in. His name was Sky Dayton, and he and I met at a time when I was becoming a very busy sell-side, mergers and acquisitions broker of Internet Service Providers ("ISPs"). When you use your Internet to send or receive an email, the message is carried by an ISP. Practically all of the smaller ones for which I found buyers – just short of 100 all told – are now part of AT&T, Verizon, Century Link and the other carriers.

The origin of the ISP dates back to 1971. The U.S. Government, frightened by the Russians' launch of Sputnik, created an agency called ARPANET, which linked computers owned by the Department of Defense throughout the U.S. An employee of ARPANET by the name of Ray Tomlinson sent an experimental message between two computers in the same room and he chose the @ symbol for his email. The @ symbol is sometimes called the "elephant-trunk A" which goes by the phrase *snabel-a* in Danish or *aapenstartje* ("the little monkey's tale) in Dutch. Of course emojis – those cartoon characters to describe emotions that CEOs and kindergartners are using – are the new hot orthographic addition.

When I became a sell-side M&A broker of ISPs, News Corporation called me to sell its national backbone that it shared ownership with Mitsubishi. On hindsight, bad move, as it could today be sending 20th Century Fox and Fox Searchlight movies downs its own pipes. Sky Dayton wanted to buy it for EarthLink, and that's the first assignment that he gave us. The second was raising expansion capital for EarthLink.

Our first meeting was at Café Mocha in Los Angeles, a coffee shop that Sky owned. It was painted dark brown and orange, very grunge.

"How old are you?" I asked.

"Twenty-three," he said.

"And I gather you finished college?"

"No, I never went."

"Why?"

"Because I didn't think that college had much to teach me," he said.

Sky's father was a sculptor, he said, and his mother a dancer and poet. Shortly after his birth in New York City, the family moved to Los Angeles. He lived for a time with his maternal grandparents. His grandfather, David DeWitt, who was an IBM Fellow, played a huge part in introducing Sky to technology and computers.

At the age of 9, Sky got his first computer, a Sinclair ZX81. He learned to program in BASIC on this early machine. At age 16, Sky graduated from the Delphian School, a private boarding school in Oregon, which uses study methods developed by L. Ron Hubbard. He got a job at an entertainment advertising firm where he became exposed to Apple Macintosh hardware and digital imaging software and soon managed the digital imaging department. Sky then moved on to a larger advertising agency, Mednick & Associates, where he held a similar role until he was 18.

In late 1990, at the age of 19, Sky and a friend raised money from family and friends and opened Mocha Gallery, an art gallery and coffee house in L.A. After six months, they change the name to Café Mocha and got rid of the art business. The trendy Café Mocha was written up in the *Los Angeles Times, Vogue* and *GQ Magazine,* and was featured on MTV's "House of Style." He and his partner soon took over another coffeehouse called Joe Café in Studio City, California.

In 1993, Sky heard about the Internet. After spending 80 hours trying to get his Macintosh computer to log in, he finally got connected. Realizing that the Internet was likely to become the next mass medium, in 1994, he decided to start EarthLink. He was 23 years old. In search of startup capital, he approached Kevin O'Donnell, father of a childhood friend, followed by Bob Kavner, Chip Lacy and George Soros, a legendary investor and philanthropist. What he was overcoming in selecting a handful of well-known validators, was his youthfulness and lack of experience in building a major telecom company. And he did it well.

Sky began in 600 square feet of space in an office in Los Angeles. By leasing pipe from UUNET, a national backbone, EarthLink was able to provide national service. EarthLink competed with AOL primarily, and quickly grew to $1 billion in annual revenues. Sky took the company public, exited with $120 million while still in his twenties, and founded Boingo, a WIFI hot spot aggregator which busy travelers use in major airports throughout the world.

One of my youngest ISP clients was a Cleveland lad who had just turned 16. He was running his ISP out of his bedroom in his parents' house. They didn't know it. He hid the servers under his bed. When he made a new sale, he would jump out of the back window, hop into his older brother's car, and drive to the new customer's house and do the install and the training in getting to the Internet. His customer service was the best I had ever seen, all because he loved to drive, as 16 year olds do. I was writing a column for *Forbes* at the time, and Jim Michaels, the senior editor, liked this story and inserted the line, "…the lad's service is certainly better than AOL's." Steve Case wrote me. He wasn't pleased.

The importance of validators cannot be over-stated, particularly if you are an entrepreneur without a strong track record in business. You can put the names of your validators on an Advisory Board. Making them Directors when you are just a start-up, is not the right thing to do, because insurance for board members, known as Directors and Officers Liability Insurance, or ("D&O") is quite expensive, something on the order of $6,000 per year per million dollars of coverage for each Director. They can be Advisors, and give you the benefit of their experience while demonstrating to smart investors that you have validators.

Who Else is in it?

What the investor is saying with this direct question, is this: "I understand what you are supplying. But, who is demanding it? Who is demonstrating hunger? Show me the hunger?" This is often a tough question for a start-up, because most start-ups represent the Supply curve and the entrepreneurs believe that Demand will show up. Now, we know that Steve Jobs conceived of the iPhone without a demand curve for it – but, that is rare.

Bill Gates and Paul Allen founded Microsoft Corporation in 1975 and were working on writing an operating system for the emerging personal computer industry. In 1980, IBM Corporation decided to enter the PC market and it went looking for an operating system. It sent a team to Pacific Grove, CA to meet with Gary Kildall, founder of Digital Research Corp., who had a proven operating system; but, Dr. Kildall was out flying his seaplane and did not choose to come down from the sky to license his software. So, the IBMers journeyed up to Seattle and asked Bill Gates and Paul Allen if they would license their operating system, which they did not have. Shrewdly, Gates agreed to a license of MS-DOS which he purchased from Seattle Computer Products, Inc. with money he received as a down payment from IBM on an imputed license of what Gates named PC DOS, while Microsoft held onto the mother ship, known as MS DOS, which all of us who do not use Apple computers run our PC's with. With his cleverness, Gates held onto the most valuable asset since the discovery of oil, and happily has become, with his wife, Melinda, one of the greatest philanthropic organizations having gifted $30 billion thus far to very needy people and places. With IBM as a licensee, Microsoft easily secured a round of venture capital.

Risk Aversion:

To answer the first three questions – How much can I make? How much can I lose? And, how do I get my money out? – a brief description of the angel capital and venture capital business models is necessary. I will refer to them as venture capital funds, as some of them do in fact back start-ups, which is the role of angel capital funds. In reading the Web sites of venture capital funds, you will see that some of them say they invest at the seed level, which is quite risky. To begin, please refer to Figure 2, Graph of the Five Risks of a Start-up Company.

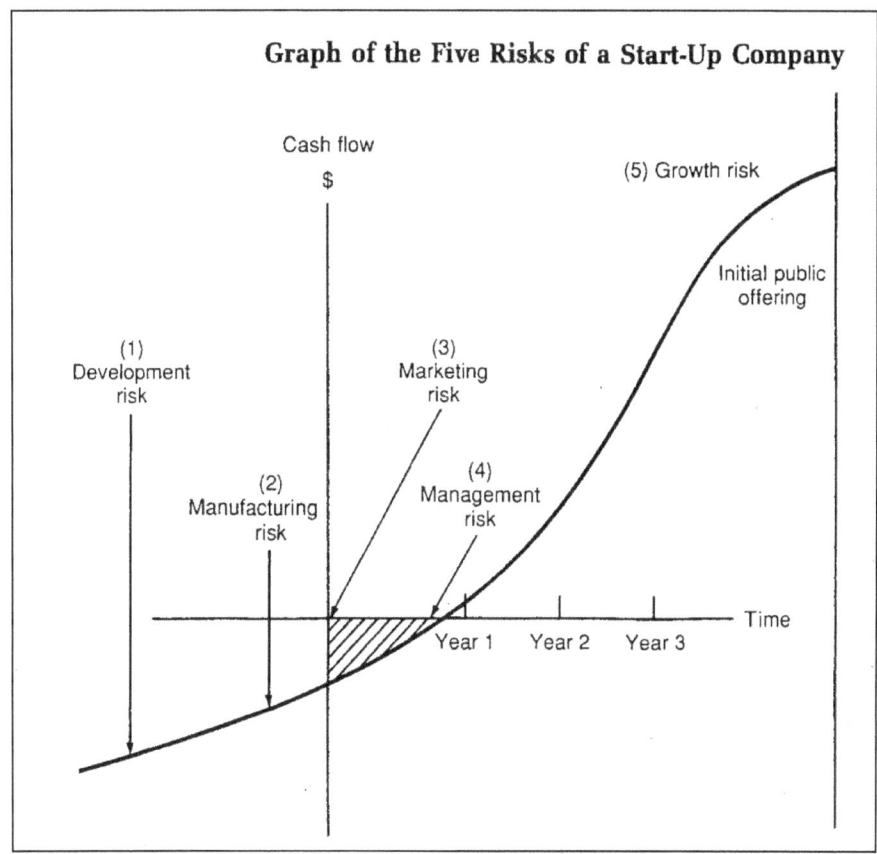

Figure 2

Typically, the entrepreneur takes the development risk, which is conceiving the idea (the Supply factor) to meet the hunger or the pain or the need of thousands or millions of people (the Demand factor). This is done via research and thankfully Google, Bing, Yahoo and Wikipedia have made search a less expensive process than ever before. I am also a big fan of industry magazines, because they often describe a big need in their industry. In two recent cases, I needed to measure the size – the "P" factor – of two industries – commercial refrigeration equipment and California's plan to kill the gas tax and replace it with a road usage tax. The latter would affect long haul trucking companies which use the highways more than families who travel to schools, shopping centers and to their employment. I found lots of data in journals published by the gasoline and convenience store journals on the subject of higher taxes for their primary customer, the long haul trucker. In the case of commercial refrigeration equipment – the glass doors that we open for milk and ice cream at our favorite supermarkets – new Federal regulations to reduce carbon emissions have been proposed and will require retro-fitting all of those refrigerated containers. These two changes create what I call Demand, or Hunger, or to the industries that must retrofit, the word is Pain.

The next step in the "S" curve, which is the Graph above, is the manufacturing risk. It is generally paid for by family and friends of the entrepreneur in what has come to be known as the Family and Friends round. This could be $50,000 or $100,000 depending on the complexity of the prototype that needs to be built. If it is a software program and the prototype is an algorithm, thanks to the digital age that we live in, this task can be farmed out to TopTal, an online algorithm service. For a company name, there is the dictionary, or behindthename.com, for the meaning of Greek gods' and goddesses' names ("Nike" is the Greek goddess of victory in contests; "Uber" means "to an excessive degree"; and I recently chose "Ostara" for a new business, because of its definition: in German, it means "Spring rising."). If a logo is needed in order to give meaning to the company's name, I found great success in the creation of a logo for Ostara Technology Co., Inc. at 99design.com, where graphic artists from around the world bid against one another to create the best logo design. The cost is a mere $299.00 for absolutely elegant work. And to build the social network itself, there are many custom shops who will seek to charge you an arm and a leg, but Fiverr can build one for you for $100.00. You can add the bells and whistles with the help of a local geek. I register all my domain names with Catalog.com, because I helped them launch years ago and have a small ownership position. GoDaddy.com is much less expensive and does a fine job.

To test the Demand for the product or service you have created in the Manufacturing Risk stage, you will need to do some market research. If you have found a product such as kombucha, the tea that tastes like apple vinegar but has certain alleged healing properties, there are several start-ups competing for leadership and shelf space. The kombucha entrepreneurs use focus groups where people from different walks of life are brought into a conference room to taste and discuss a new product. Adler-Weiner Research Co., Inc. with offices in Chicago and Los Angeles, is one of the leading focus group companies in the U.S. A typical focus group study for an entrepreneurial company is around $7,500, according to Andy Weiner, with whom I discussed the process a few months ago for a client of mine with a new mobile app.

Entrepreneurs seek "testimonials" from potential customers, which are relatively weak elements of a Demand curve. Stronger than testimonials are "pilots," which are actual tests of a product or service by a potential customer or client. For an entrepreneur to say to a wizened venture capitalist, "We have completed a pilot with Intel Corp., which has agreed to use our platform, but we need $1 million to hire the twenty-five software engineers to expand the algorithms," well, that is a strong statement. The venture capitalist is likely to respond with, "If I have your permission to contact Intel, and if they verify what you just said, then sure, we'll write you a check."

But, you may not be able to crack open a pilot with Intel because you lack an Advisory Board member who has a contact there. In fact, you may not have an Advisory Board at all. Then you have to shoot with a shot gun instead of a rifle and the best place to do that is LinkedIn. It is home to 117,000,000 people in business who want to be found, and who tell quite a bit about themselves. You can pitch them on LinkedIn with an "inmail," LinkedIn's version of email.

The bottom line is in order to generate serious amounts of upfront financing, to get to the Marketing Stage of the "S" curve, it will be incumbent upon you to demonstrate Demand for your product or service. Venture capital will not flock to your start-up without evidence of a Demand curve beginning to form for the Supply curve that you built and are ready to market.

In his book, *"Originals,"* Viking Press, 2016, Adam Grant writes, "...originals form alliances to advance their goals [in order to] overcome barriers that prevent coalitions from succeeding. By definition, most efforts to change the status quo involve a movement by a minority group to challenge a majority." Grant goes on to explain why a change-maker, which he calls an "original" will often seek to form an alliance with someone or with a group that she has always considered an opponent, in order to crack open a Demand curve for her new disruptive and pain solving service.

Risk Aversion:

And now back to our originally scheduled program: How to answer the questions, "How much can I make? How much can I lose? And How do I get my money back?" There are angel capital funds, venture capital funds and seed capital divisions within venture capital funds. I will lump them into one category – venture capital funds for simplicity. They are risk averse investors. The reason lies in the numbers.

Their target rate of return is 10.0x (ten times their investment dollars) in five years and 5.0x in three years. You can see that these times-money-earned ratios translate nicely into percentage return on investment ("ROI") in Figure 2.2 following entitled Target Rates of Return of a Typical Venture Capital Fund. They compute to 70.0% to 90.0% per annum.

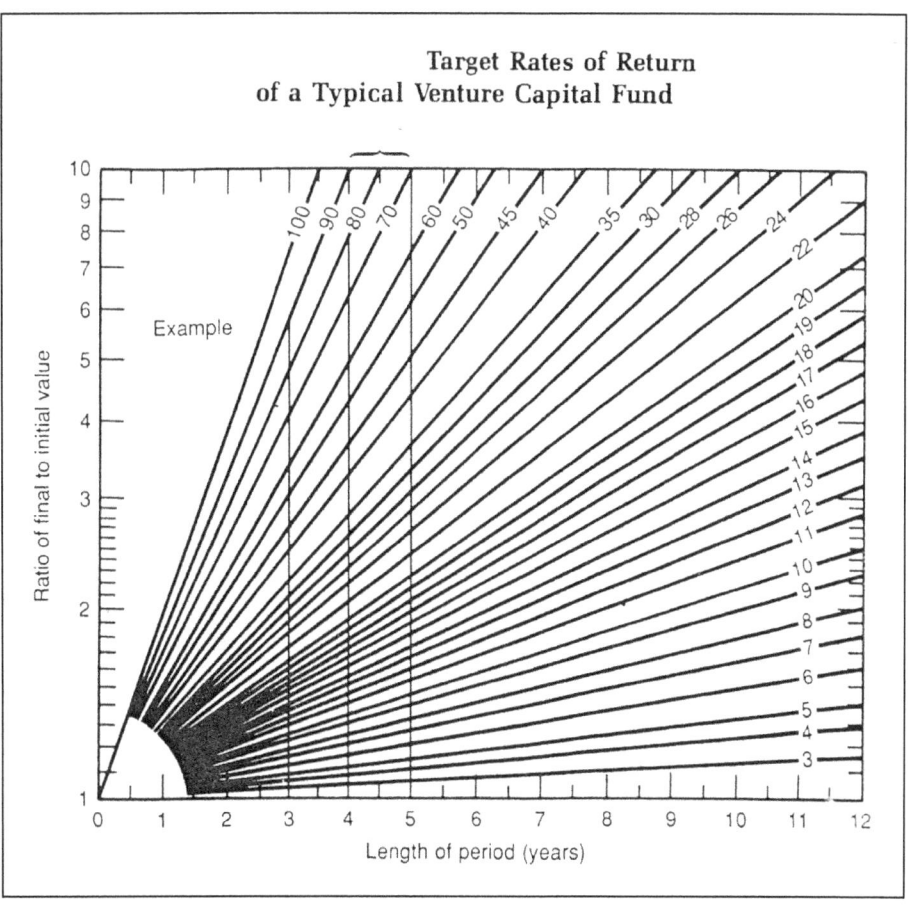

Figure 3

Venture capital funds are partnerships. The people you will pitch are the General Partners and the providers of the capital with which they invest are the Limited Partners. The ownership of the Fund is typically that the Limited Partners will receive 80% of the capital gains and the General Partners will receive 20%. Losses are shared the same way. The Limited Partners pay the General Partners 1.5% to 2.0% to manage their money. Thus, in a venture capital fund with $100 million, the six or eight people who seek really good investments to make 10 or 15 investments have $1.5 million to $2.0 million for salaries and due diligence costs.

The beauty of the venture capital business is that one home run can make up for five or six wipe-outs. One of the greatest home runs of the modern era is Facebook. Let's say your venture capital fund was approached by Mark Zuckerberg ten years ago for a $1 million investment, and you bought 5.0% of the Facebook's common stock, valuing the company at $20 million post-funding. ("Post-funding" is the expression of a valuation made by a venture capital fund, and a word pair that you might want to start using to demonstrate awareness of how the game is played.) Another word is "scalability," which means an early-stage company that can grow quickly by word-of-mouth marketing, digital marketing with Google Ad Words and pitching messages to the profiled people rented to you by Facebook.) So, after several more capital raises by Facebook, your 5.0% ownership has been diluted down to 1.0%. Facebook is publicly held now (symbol: FB) and has a market capitalization of $331 billion.

Your 1.0% is worth $3.3 billion. All of the nation's 150,000 employees of the nation's 2,200 venture capital funds dream of hitting it out of the park with a Facebook-sized win. But, those come around very rarely. In a typical seven- to ten-year partnership, the venture capital fund will make 15 investments, of which three or four will yield 10.0x or more, three or four will wipe out and six or seven will languish in the $10 million to $40 million range, lacking serious scalability. If the venture capital fund's management has been sending its winners to the initial public offering ("IPO") market, it might be able to lean on its investment bankers to take a few of the languishing companies public. That form of leaning on somewhat sycophantic investment bankers is sardonically called "Go broke or go public."

But, look at the math in the example just provided: Let's assume $400 million of capital gains, $27 million of wipe-outs and $30 million of languishers. The net capital gain is $400 million minus $57 million equals a net gain of $343 million. Of that amount, the limited partners receive 80% or $274 million. The general partners receive $68 million. Let's say there are eight people sharing the $68 million over an eight-year period, or $8.5 million per year, and more than $1 million per employee. But, to achieve that relatively high level of income, venture capitalists must be risk averse. They must become surgical with their due diligence; granular in their review of the opportunity, making sure there is a real differentiator to the business and a moat to prevent competitors from denying scalability to the company they intend to invest in. Some venture capital funds hire due diligence companies, one of the best-known of which is Navigant, Inc., headquartered in Chicago, but with dozens of offices throughout the U.S. and Latin America. As Richard Dumler, General Partner of Milestone Venture Partners, New York puts it, "The question you failed to ask the entrepreneur is the one that will cause you to lose money on the deal." Thus, there is no way to hurry up the venture capital fund examining your deal. It takes time to close an investment with them.

The Exit:

Venture capitalists want to know the most likely exit before they invest. There two primary exit routes: the IPO and sale to a synergistic company. The IPO route is hit or miss, meaning sometimes the IPO window is open, but most of the time it is closed. It was open in 2014 – 15 and it is closed in 2016. The collapse of oil prices has put a lot of pressure on institutional portfolios, nearly all of which hold quite a few oil and gas stocks. They're choking on oil and gas, and thus can't buy new digital companies' publicly-issued shares.

Thus, the favored exit route is to find a buyer for the fund's companies. To achieve that, the companies become "irritants" to larger companies in the industry. For example, if the upstart company finds a niche in the HVAC ("heating, ventilating and air conditioning") market, for example, it has developed a mobile app to enable home owners to shut off heat and electricity remotely to save on energy costs, a larger HVAC company such as Siemens or Johnson Controls might pay a premium over the smaller companies' revenues to enter the digital age by acquiring a mobile app energy monitoring company.

When Nuance won a contract from the Bing, the Microsoft search engine, to enable it return the right answer to a search question, rather than hundreds of answers as Google does, it approached a portfolio company of mine, Cognition Technologies, Inc., Los Angeles, CA, which owns a natural language search engine, and acquired it at a handsome premium over revenues.

It is a very good idea when you are calling on venture capitalists to know the names of likely acquirers of your company and to list them at the investor meetings.

CHAPTER SIX

WRITING THE BUSINESS PLAN/FUNDING MEMORANDUM

The younger employees of the venture capital world like to see investor decks rather than the old-fashioned PPMs, and thus I advise it. If you are not good with graphic art, pie charts and doing your own operating statement projections, you can hire Fiverr to do the job for very little money. I have used them to convert my instructions, known in the trade as list of assumptions, for a set of 36 month operating statement projections for a fee of $25.00.

The subject matter of the Business Plan, which is actually the same as a Funding Memorandum, except the latter has the valuation information in it.

The infrastructure of the Business Plan is the PERT Chart. PERT stands for Program Evaluation and Research Tool, and it was developed by the Rand Corporation in the 1950's. In the PERT Chart the description of the task to be completed is written down in the time period in which it must be done. The person on the team to whom the task is assigned is attached to the task and the time period. In Figure 4 in which I have presented a sample PERT Chart, you will see that the team responsible for the Product has five tasks to achieve; the Equipment team has three tasks to achieve, the Plant team has two tasks to achieve; and so forth.

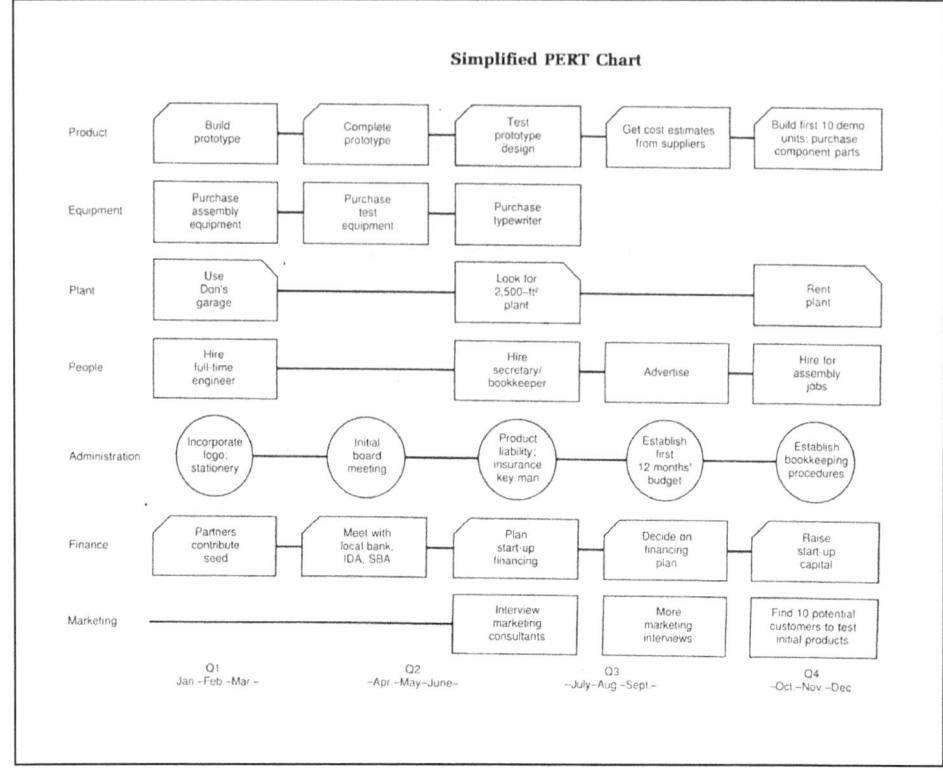

Figure 4

The PERT Chart will yield up dollar amounts, and these will include the cash expenditures up to product launch and first revenues. It could take 12 months or 15 months or 18 months to build the underpinnings of the new company, but these are critical months when the team members begin to pull together. It wouldn't be surprising if a team member is replaced. After all, Ringo Starr wasn't the Beatles' original drummer. The launch is then added to the 36 month operating statement projections with sales slowly building in what is known as the "Hockey Stick." The Hockey Stick makes this statement to investors, "Our Company's sales are down here at the toe of the hockey stick, but with your money, we can grow sales to the top of the handle of the hockey stick. In Figure 5, you will see a sample Hockey Stick.

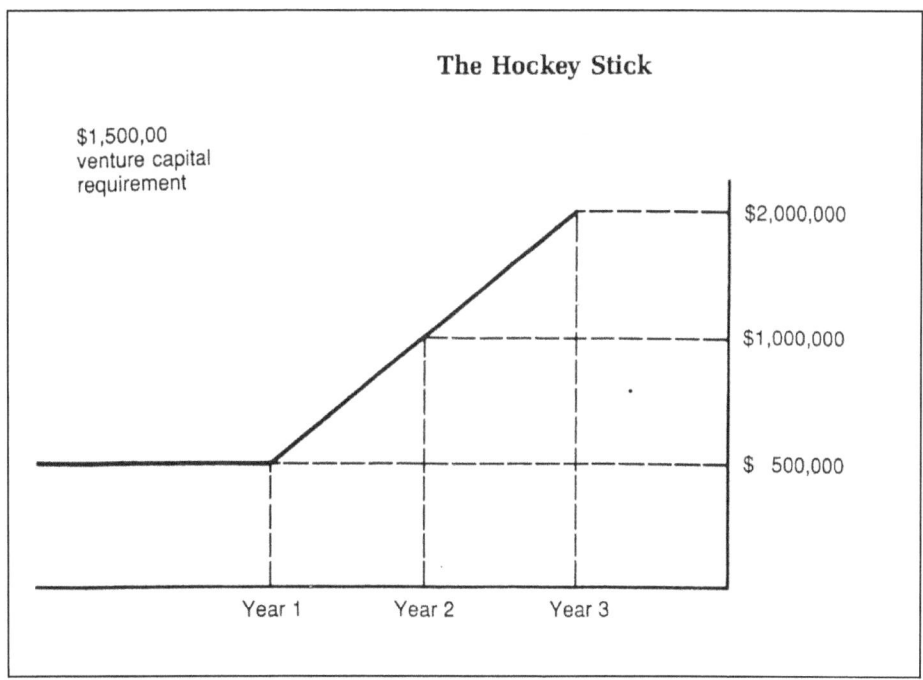

Figure 5

It is the angle of the Hockey Stick that the entrepreneur and the investor are focused on. An angle of 45 degrees is relatively rapid growth. An angle of 60 degrees or a larger number lacks credibility, because businesses do not often grow that rapidly. However, since venture capital funds have relatively short lives, they like to see higher degrees. If they "buy" the story of the start-up team, they might offer more capital in order to hasten the sales growth.

If the entrepreneurs present a hockey stick of less than 45 degrees, it will not impress the investors, because it is just too slow a ramp up and they are not seeking to have their capital put to work that slowly. Again, with 2,200 U.S. venture capital funds, 500 or so angel capital funds and 220 angel groups, there is quite a bit of capital seeking to be moved from their banks to the banks of the start-up companies; so, asking for more capital and angling the hockey stick a bit higher than 45 degrees is going to bring you more offers for funding than will a more conservative approach.

Use of Proceeds: A critical section of the Business Plan/Funding Memorandum is the description of how the investor's money will be used. An entrepreneurial team called on me several months ago and showed me a business plan with a Use of Proceed section that showed the purchase of three new desks for $10,000 apiece. I got a little enthusiastic in showing them the door. Entrepreneurs can put three doors and six wooden horses together for their desks, and buy three chairs at the Salvation Army for $2.00 apiece. The inexpensive desk was good enough for Dr. Henry Singleton, the founder of Teledyne. Warren Buffett considered Singleton the best manager in America. He made 130 acquisitions with one assistant, and a partner, George Roberts, who oversaw their operations. Sales grew to $3 billion in 14 years and Teledyne's stock price jumped from $3.00 to $300 over the same period. I met him in his office when I was representing Dr. Woog in the sale of Broxodent, the first electric toothbrush company. Only three people could sit in Singleton's office at the same time, and he sat behind a sheet metal grey reclaimed Navy desk. It probably cost him $5.00 at one of their auctions of decommissioned objects.

The expenditures that investors like to see in the Use of Proceeds section are marketing related. If some of their capital is needed to finish the product, you could be shown the door also; because you are asking them to take the manufacturing risk. They do not do that. Bear in mind that venture capitalists are fiduciaries of the money entrusted to them by pension funds, endowment funds, insurance companies and family offices. Therefore, a misuse of their money will make them extremely upset at you. Sticking to the Use of Proceeds is the wisest move, and if you have to make a material departure, notifying the investor in advance and obtaining approval is the best path.

Valuation:

The cherry on the top of the cake of the Business Plan/Funding Memorandum is the section on valuation. For this, I use Capital IQ, a subsidiary of Standard & Poors, Inc. Capital IQ captures the values of transactions – financings and acquisitions. You can dial-up all of the recent financings and acquisitions of mobile app companies or software solutions providers to the enterprise market, and come up with the multiples of sales at which companies such as yours are raising capital or being acquired. Notice that I didn't say multiples of earnings. It seems that sales are the new metrics. If for example, Capital IQ says that companies such as yours are being acquired at a multiple of 5.0x trailing revenues if under $20 million in sales and 7.0x trailing revenues if over $20 million in sales, you would be wise to move your Hockey Stick in the third year up to $25 million in sales. Venture capitalists love to hang their hat on Capital IQ's numbers. If you are in a university while launching your company, your school is probably paying for your Capital IQ subscription.

Let's put some numbers to the valuation and the raise. If your PERT Chart works and if your 36 month Operating Statement Projections show a deep S-Curve deficit, similar to the one in Figure 6 below, of a maximum cumulative cash deficit of $2,500,000, your capital raise should assume some things not occurring on time, and the ask should be $3,000,000. Then, if the third year revenues are $5,000,000 and the multiple that acquirers pay for companies similar to yours with $5,000,000 in revenues is 5.0x, or $25,000,000; then, it is reasonable for you to value the company at perhaps two-thirds of $25,000,000, or $16,500,000. When that number is divided into the $3,000,000 raise the offer of ownership to the investor is 18.8% ownership.

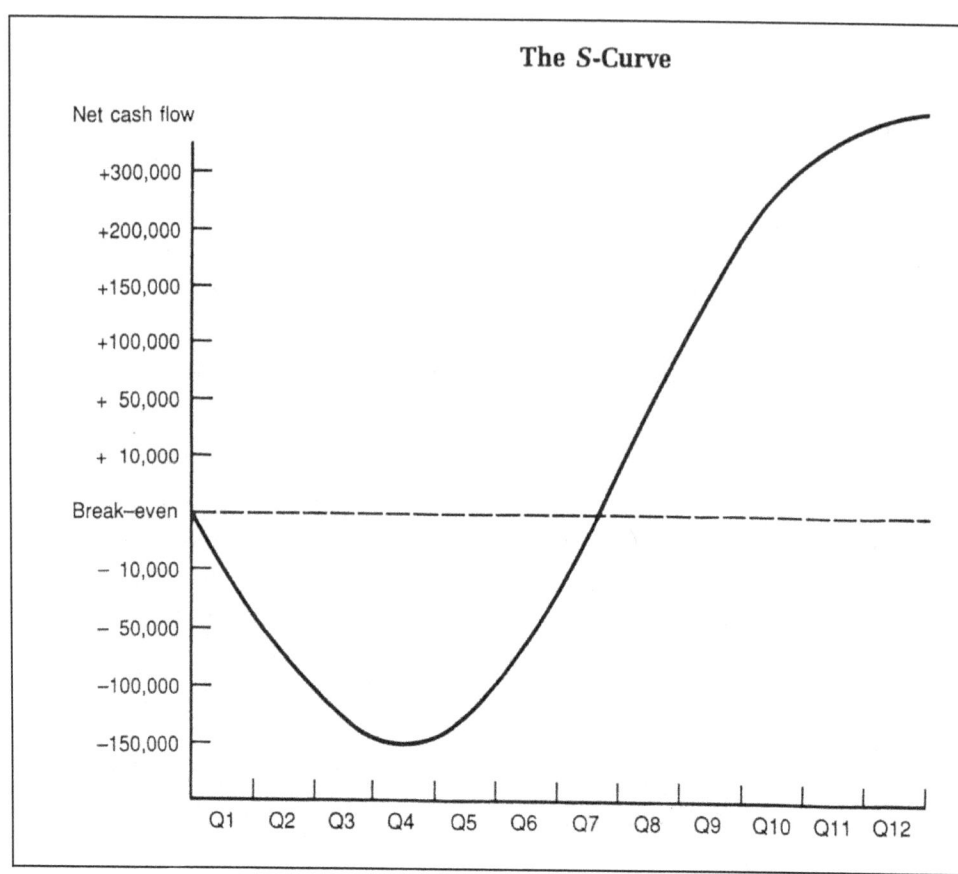

Figure 6

The investor will likely push back, and ask for some more ownership; but, that's a good sign. The entrepreneur should take the counter-offer back to his or her team and not be rushed, even if the company's bank account is down to fifty cents. The counter-offer from the investor is probably created by the fund's Investment Committee, with instructions to, "See if you can get another 10 points, but settle for 5."

When the entrepreneur counters the counter, it should be to give the investor another five percentage points. It will come back many times that number if the company is as good as its team mates thinks it is. Plus, there is much more to launching a company than securing the capital.

CHAPTER SEVEN

SOURCES OF UPFRONT FINANCING

Thankfully there are alternatives to venture capital funding. Some of them are clear-cut sources that obviate the need for venture capital, and others are symbiotic with venture capital.

Family and Friends:

The structure of the family and friends financing, in my opinion, should be a convertible promissory note, with the conversion rate set at a discount to the first institutional capital raise, be it angel or venture capital. The note should bear interest of course, but at a low rate, say 5.0%, and payable at the end of twelve months. This should give you enough time to move the company forward to a point where it can raise venture capital. But, if takes another few months, you can ask permission of the family and friends to grant you a delay until you pay interest on their note. What I like about the convertible promissory note is that it provides an option to the lender to ask for his or her money back rather than convert into the company's common stock. Plus, it pays a little bit of interest, which substitutes for the interest that the family member or the friend lost when he pulled his money of that place and loaned it to you.

Then, when the venture capital fund invests at say, $1.00 per share, the family member or the friend can invest at 80 cents per share, or alternatively, ask for his principal back. At that time, the family member of the friend will very likely ask you to tell him or truthfully, do you think he or she should convert? This is the moment of truth. If you believe your family member or your friend will truly make a profit on his or her investment, then you should encourage them to convert into the company's common stock. If you don't think that's the case, then you probably haven't convinced an institutional investor to invest in your company, and in that case, it would be the most truthful route to say that you will take a job somewhere to pay back the family member or friend's money.

There are convertible promissory note examples on the Web. One of the best is at www.template.com. A lawyer might charge you $5,000 to draft one, and there it is on the Web for free.

Angel Clubs:

In the mid-1980s Thomas P. Murphy, a *Forbes* columnist on the topic of venture capital conceived the notion of the angel capital club and the five-minute forum. He invited wealthy friends to a dinner in a Stamford, CT hotel conference room one evening each month. The investors would eat, then scoot their chairs around and listen to five-minute oral pitches by entrepreneurs, which Tom called the five minute forum. If an entrepreneur's story interested one or two members of the audience, they would ask to speak with him or her later that evening, or in the next few days at their offices. Tom did not charge for this service, as it would have seemed tacky to him. But, he did see that it could replicated in many more cities than Stamford, CT and Santa Fe, NM where I had been running a replica since 1981.

Tom became ill around 1985 and asked me to take an interview with Jim Michaels at *Forbes* to become his replacement columnist and to take over the angel capital club movement. I passed the Jim Michaels interview at lunch in Greenwich Village and began writing a bi-monthly column; and I began assisting other cities in launching their angel clubs. I traveled to many cities in the U.S. and to Malaysia, Singapore, South Africa, Israel, Puerto Rico and elsewhere launching these clubs, without seeking compensation.

I was frequently asked to be the guest speaker at these new club launches. I used to open my talk this way: "When do you think the first wheelbarrow was invented? Throw out some dates." And the answers would fly up to me, "Ten thousand years ago. "Five thousand years ago." And so forth. Then, I would say, "And when did the luggage industry first put wheels on suitcases?" Everyone was stunned. "The answer is 1970." I would pause and say, "So, that should give you an idea of how many innovations there out there that entrepreneurs haven't thought of yet, but will. And they will bring a bunch of them into this club."

Back at the Santa Fe Angel Club, we launched several businesses, the largest of which was Amtech Corp., developer of the E-Z Pass. Dr. Gary Seawright, a Pharmacologist at Los Alamos National Laboratories in nearby Los Alamos, had invented a transformer in the form of an RFID chip. The receiver would be held in the hand of a pig farmer. He could locate his pigs anywhere by putting the chip in their ear and pinging it from time to time.

That plan was DOA, because it would have added twenty-five cents to the cost of the pig. But, Gary raised some capital at my club, and a bunch of us started working on a new Demand curve. The real Hunger came from owners of cargo ships on the high seas. By placing an RFID chip on the chips, they could be spotted from cameras in satellites circling the earth, and in the event of a hijacking, the ship owners could immediately signal for help.

The RFID chip that is now on 27,000,000 car and truck windshields in the U.S. and a like number in Europe, was not an easy sell. But, Gary tried to topple the largest owner of toll gates in the U.S. with the toughest people managing them – the Tibor Bridge and Tunnel Authority of New York, Connecticut and New Jersey. The people who run this "Authority" are tough and difficult to govern, precisely because they are the law. If you read Robert Caro's 1975 book, Pulitzer Prize winning book, *"Power Broker: Robert Moses and the Fall of New York,"* you will see how Moses used his power to create roads, place toll booths on some and beautiful overpasses on some, roads like the Taconic Parkway that takes New Yorkers upstate. The power brokers who Moses created installed their cousins, their uncles, their nieces, and their nephews to collect tolls all over the tri-state area, and they were strongly disinclined to remove them and replace them with E-Z Pass receivers. But, Gary, a shy man with tons of intellectual capital, knew he was doing the right thing for the citizens of the area who needed to get to airports, to get to work and to get home more quickly. He persisted, and the E-Z Pass was launched.

It initially created 164 tech jobs in Santa Fe, and as you know, one new tech job created 4.0x in additional jobs from teachers to dental assistants to beauticians. Today, Amtech Corp. has been split into two companies, one for the cargo ships and the other for cars and trucks. Each company employs roughly 10,000 people. A disruptive and pain solving company launched from an angel club in a small mountain town known for its artists and restaurants. I ran the club for 11 years, on the third Thursday of each month at a conference room at the Santa Fe Hilton. One night in 1992, I looked out at the audience and it was 95% lawyers trolling for business like Alfred Hitchcock's movie *"The Birds,"* pecking away at entrepreneurs who were seeking capital flowing in, not flowing out to lawyers. I shut it down.

But, the wave was breaking all over the world. In the U.S. today there are 13,000 angels hearing pitches at 240 angel clubs. The angels are older gentlemen for the most part, but there are some ladies, and of course some are more active than others. For example, the Desert Angels in Tucson, AZ www.desertangels.org, have 90 members. Formed in 2000, the Desert Angels have invested $37 million in 85 entrepreneurial companies. They are one of the most active angel groups.

The method of presenting to the angel clubs has become more stratified as well. The clubs want presentations to come to them on one page, like a teaser, of the kind I described earlier, but with smaller print, in three columns and with more facts. They will accept the presentations in one of two formats, Gust or Proseeder. To see what a Gust and a Proseeder presentation look like, you should visit www.gust.com and www.proseeder.com. The Cowtown Angels in Texas, the Empire Angels in New York State and the Desert Angels in Tucson, AZ prefer Proseeder. I believe it is a more conventional submission format.

I will tell you that if you go the angel group route, you will be waiting for events to occur beyond your control. You cannot rush the angel groups. They have their own procedures. For example, after submitting your Gust or Proseeder application, you will be notified if the angel group has accepted you to present at their next lunch or dinner meeting. That could be two months from your date of submittal. If you make the cut and actually present to the group, they will get back to you if they wish to go into a due diligence process with you. That could take a couple of weeks. If you pass the due diligence, you're in.

I went through this process with a client of mine, CollisionHub.com, a social network for people and businesses involved in the unhappy process of fixing repaired cars. The body shops were over charging the car owners, the parts vendors were over charging the body shops, the auto insurance companies were under-funding the car owners. Nobody was happy with anybody. So, where's the hunger? Kristen Felder, a young lady who had worked in an auto body shop and for Nationwide Insurance Co., and who lived in Jonesboro, AK. The pain was in every crevice and paint shop in the industry. Kristen's ideas were to get the players onto a social network and have them talk about themselves, their families, their barbecues, their dogs, their golf games and everything they could come up with. It actually worked. Friendships sprung up, recipes for carrot cake were passed from friend to friend, players who were once gouging each other met for golf. And, the advertisers have flocked to Kristen's social network, www.collisionhub.com. The Arkansas Angel Club provided the capital to launch Collison Hub, and it was one of the faster processes I have been through. The Winthrop Rockefeller Fund keeps the Arkansas Angel Club well-funded, paying for due diligence, for instance.

My advice to you if you are in start-up mode is to proceed with two or three angel clubs that are in your neck of the woods, while at the same time calling on angel and venture funds; if your business model fits some of the non-equity strategies for raising capital, pursue them as well. And pursue them with zeal. Zealotry pays in the start-up business. You may have six or eight irons in the fire at one time and if that doesn't work, expand your shopping list to 16. J.K. Rowling, the author of the Harry Potter series, which has sold 400 million copies, wrote a new manuscript under the pseudonym Robert Galbraith, and she circulated to publishers in the U.K. Dozens turned her down; and one advised her to take a course in writing. She said, "I wasn't going to stop until I had contacted every single publisher in the English-speaking world."

In Table 2 following, I have provide a handsome sampling of the most active angel clubs in the U.S.

Table 2: MANY OF THE MOST ACTIVE ANGEL CLUBS IN THE U.S. ARRANGED BY STATE

Angel Group Regions:	Name of Representative Angel Group	Send Business Plan To:
California	• Sand Hill Angels LLC - Sunnyvale, CA • Band of Angels - Menlo Park, CA • San Joaquin Angels - Stockton, CA • Sand Hill Angels LLC - Sunnyvale, CA	• info@sandhillangels.com • contact@bandangels.com • mplovnick@pacific.edu • info@sandhillangels.com
Great Lakes	• Cornerstone Angels - Northbrook, IL • Silicon Pastures - Milwaukee, WI • Urbana-Champaign Angel Network - Urbana, IL • X-Squared Angels - Columbus, OH	Fill out Application
Mid-Atlantic	• 757 Angels Network - Virginia Beach, VA • New Richmond Ventures - Richmond, VA • Hivers and Strivers - Great Falls, VA • K Street Capital - Washington, DC	• info@richmondventures.com
Midwest/ Great Plains	• Chicago ArchAngels - Chicago, IL • Nebraska Angels Inc - Lincoln, NE • Bluegrass Angels - Lexington, KY • Enterprise Angel Group LLC - Louisville, KY	Fill out Application
New England	• Boston Harbor Angels - Boston, MA • Ocean State Angels - Providence, RI • Walnut Venture Associates - Wellesley Hills, MA • ECS Angels - Bar Harbor, ME	Fill out Application
New York	• Astia Angels - New York, NY (and San Francisco) • Eastern New York Angels - Albany, NY • LAVAN Project - New York, NY • Rochester Angel Network - Rochester, NY	Fill out Application
Pacific Northwest	• Bellingham Angel Investors - Bellingham, WA • Frontier Angel Fund - Kalispell, MT • Oregon Angel Fund - Portland, OR • Seattle Angels - Seattle, WA	• jj@bellinghamangelinvestors.com • lynn@oregonangelfund.com
Southeast	• Asheville Angels - Asheville, NC • New World Angels - Boca Raton, FL • South Coast Angel Fund - New Orleans, LA • Miami Innovation Fund, Inc. - Miami, FL	Fill out Application
Southwest	• Arizona Tech Investors (ATI) - Tempe, AZ • Desert Angels - Tucson, AZ • New Mexico Angels Inc - Albuquerque, NM	• jcgoulka@atif-az.org • morrisonr@quest.net • jchavez@nmangels.com
Texas	• Aggie Angels - College Station, TX • Research Valley Funds, LLC - College Station, TX • Cowtown Angels - Ft. Worth, TX • North Texas Angel Network - Dallas, TX	• james@researchvalleyfunds.com • cowtownangels@techfortworth.org • chuck@northtexasangelnetwork.org
West	• REES Capital LLC - South Jordan, UT • Hawaii Angels - Honolulu, HI • Angel Capital Group - Denver, CO • Sierra Angels - Incline Village, NV	Fill out Application

Angel Capital Funds:

More than 800 start-ups were funded in 2015 in New York City alone. The majority of them were social networks and mobile apps. That is a stunning number, and demonstrates the power of digital marketing, which is the newest industry to capture lower Manhattan. New York has always had most of the nation's advertising agencies, so when Google moved to the Chelsea section of New York City in 2012, and bought the biggest building in the city, the old Port Authority building, Facebook took over a nearly equal building across the street from Google. These events brought Publicis, JWT, Omnicom and all of the vintage ad agencies to this area, known as the Flat Iron District. Young people who were starting social networks and mobile apps moved to the flatiron district, and they were followed by roughly 100 angel capital funds. It is difficult to say if the track record of the Flat Iron District angel funds has been off the charts, average or terrible. But, they have certainly been active. It is possible that there are a few dollars left in their tills, and to that end and hope, I present in Table 3 a list of some of the more active Angel Funds, most of which to be sure are in New York City.

Table 3: AMERICA'S MOST ACTIVE ANGEL FUNDS

Genacast (Gil Beyda, Jordan Elpern-Waxman)
Lerer Ventures (Ken Lerer, Ben Lerer, Eric Hippeau)
IA Venture Partners (Roger Ehrenberg)
Thrive Capital (Josh Kushner)
Betaworks (John Borthwick)
Brooklyn Ventures (Charlie O'Donnell)
Metamorphic (David Hirsch)
NYCSeed (Owen Davis)
Rose Tech Ventures (David S. Rose)
Vaux les Ventures (Miles Spencer)
Zelkova Ventures (Jay Levy, Lary Scheinfeld)
Quotidian Ventures (Pedro Torres Picón)
First Round Capital (Howard Morgan, Phin Barnes, et al)
RRE (Stuart Ellman, James Robinson, et al)
Union Square Ventures (Fred Wilson, Albert Wenger, Andy Weissman, et al)
DFJ Gotham (Danny Schulz, Ross Goldstein, Thatcher Bell, et al)
Greycroft Partners (Alan Patricof, Ian Sigalow, et al)

FirstMark Capital (Lawrence Lenahan et al)
New York City Investment Fund (Maria Gotsch et al)
Milestone Venture Partners (Rich Dumler, Ed Goodman, Todd Pietri)
Chart Venture Partners (Matt McCooe et al)
GC Andersen Partners (Tom Blum et al)
Contour Venture Partners (Bob Greene)
TWJ Capital (Tom Jones)

Kickstarter, SeedInvest and Other Online Funding Sources:
Beginning on May 16, 2016, the Securities and Exchange Commission ("SEC") granted permission to anyone, accredited or not, to risk $2,000 or more per year in start-up ventures. The startup ventures on the other hand, can raise up to $1 million per year from these individuals. "For the first time, ordinary Americans will be able to go online and invest in entrepreneurs that they believe in," President Obama said when he signed the JOBS Act in 2012. It took the SEC four years to codify it. The SEC will follow the activities of five online funding companies that it has approved of: CrowdBoarders, FlashFunders, NextSeed, SeedInvest and ZacksInvest, some of which have been around doing crowdfunding for several years, without the SEC's endorsement. The interesting thing is this: there has been very little fraud in the crowdfunding arena, which is a tribute to the pioneers who began their operations with the JOBS Act, and were waiting for the SEC to say, "Let the boys play," which they did on May 16, 2016. See also, Stacy Cowley's article, "Now the Small Fry Can Swim with Sharks," New York Times, May 15, 2016.

According to the international accounting firm KPMG, $13.8 billion was invested in 653 companies in the emerging global industry called Fintech. This industry is disrupting and solving pain for a financial services industry stuck in the mud since the Great Recession of 2008 - 09. The force of change in this industry is impossible to ignore, KPMG writes, with mobile-enhanced consumers having more options than ever. The rising tide of millennials is demanding more personalized and convenient services, and millennials include entrepreneurs. There are 19 Fintech unicorns, and some are on shifting sands, such as Zenefits. Once valued at $4.5 billion, this insurance industry service company is gasping for breath. Recent bond offering by Lending Club, the largest online consumer lender, had to be repriced due to lack of buyers. The online consumer lenders have so much capital from the venture capital and public markets, that it may exceed demand. Not so with its sister, the online alternative venture capital market.

A healthy section of the Fintech revolution is the alternative venture capital world. The Great Recession of 2008 -09 scared the pants off of the U.S. Congress, whose members more frequently concern themselves with their presence and press coverage than with passing useful laws. But the JOBS Act of 2012 was signed into law by every one of them and by President Obama. It stands for Jump Start Our Business Startups and it opened to door to anybody with two nickels to rub together to fund start-ups with their cash or their credit card. In June, 2015, the U.S. Securities and Exchange Commission ("SEC") signed off on the law by reducing the costliest regulatory requirements, including being vetted by state officials. State regulators hollered and screamed, "There will be foul play," but it has not occurred.

Two Online Crowdfunding Sources Where Backers Are Rewarded With "Things":

Kickstarter is living proof that easy regulations have been good for the economy. Kickstarter, founded in Brooklyn, NY in 2009 by Perry Chen, Yancey Strickler and Charles Adler, is a global crowdfunding business. Through April, 2016 it had raised $1.9 billion in pledges from 9,400,000 backers to fund 257,000 creative projects such as movies, music, stage shows, comics, journalism, video games, technology and food-related projects. People who back Kickstarter projects are offered tangible rewards and one of a kind experiences in exchange for their pledges. The model borrows from the arts patronage world where artists go directly to their patrons to fund their work. Kickstarter charges a 5.0% fee on the total amount of funds raised. If the entrepreneur sets his goal at $30,000 or $50,000, and the goal is not met, the pledgers get their money back. If the goal is not met by the deadline, no funds are collected. Entrepreneurs from the following countries may apply for Kickstarter funding:

United States	United Kingdom	Canada
Australia	New Zealand	Denmark
Ireland	Norway	Sweden
Netherlands	Spain	France
Germany	Austria	Italy
Belgium	Luxembourg	Switzerland

Kickstarter publishes its results. As of February, 2015 there were 207,135 launched projects with 7,802 in process with a success rate of 40.0%. The total amount that had been pledged as of that date $1.5 billion. One project, a dock made for the iPhone designed by Casey Hopkins became the first Kickstarter project to exceed $1 million in pledges. Then, within an hour after that, Double Fine Productions pitched a new adventure game and it received more than $3 million in pledges. In August, 2014, the "Coolest Cooler," an icebox created by Ryan Grepper, became the most funded Kickstarter project in history with $13.8 million in funding surpassing Pebble, a watch for the iPhone and the Android, which raised $10.2 million. Other Kickstarter projects which did well on Kickstarter are the following:

- World's Best Travel Jacket, created by Baubaxx raised $9.2 million from 44,949 people
- Exploding Kittens, playing cards, created by Elan Lee, $8.8 million, from 219,382 people
- Ouya, a new video game console, Ouya, Inc., $8.6 million, from 63,416 people

- "Shenmue III," video games, Yu Suzuki, $6.3 million, 69,320 people
- Pono Music, Technology, Pono Music Team, $5.8 million, 18,219 people
- *Mystery Science Thea. 3000,*" Joel Hodgson/Shout Factory, $5.8 million, 48,270 people
- "Veronica Mars" movie, Rob Thomas, $5.7 million, 91,585 people

More than 10.0% of the films accepted by the Sundance, SXSW and Tribeca Film Festivals are projects funded by Kickstarter. A number of technology start-ups have been funded by Kickstarter, but of course they have to be products usable by the backers.

After reviewing more than two years' worth of data, Ethan Mollick of the University of Pennsylvania concluded that fraud is virtually non-existent at Kickstarter. The completion rate of projects that receive their desired level of funding is 86.0%, suggesting that commitments are generally honored. Moreover, Mr. Mollick attributes the lack of fraud to what has become known as "Linus's Law," after the originator of Linux, a free computer operating system. He explains that mass vetting would quickly expose any glitches.

Advice to entrepreneurs who plan to pitch Kickstarter: it is best to have a strong video and graphic presentation. Happily, Fiverr can work with you to prepare such a presentation for less than $300. The Mallick study also pointed out that a spelling mistake in a proposal reduces the chances of a Kickstarter funding by 13.0%. But, 90.0% of the manufacturing projects that were fully funded ended up becoming fully functional firms, according to the *Economist, July 21, 2015.*

Indiegogo Disburses the Funds as They Come In:

A competitor to Kickstarter, Indiegogo was launched by Danae Ringlemann, a Wall Street analyst who co-produced a reading of an Arthur Miller play. The performance was well-received but the actors and the producers were not paid. Ms. Ringlemann went on a journey to find a way to fund theatrical productions. With the imprimatur of JP Morgan, her Wall Street employer, she was introduced to Eric Schell and Slava

Rubin at the Haas School of Business of the University of California. Schell had previously worked with the House Theater Company in Chicago. Rubin's background was in funding research for cancer research. The threesome launched Indiegogo at the Sundance Film Festival in 2008, with a focus on film projects. It has had three fund-raising events aggregating $56.5 million from the Khosla Ventures, Metamorphic Ventures, ff Venture Capital, MHS Capital and Steve Schoettler, the co-founder of Zynga, the online game developer.

Two of the differences with Kickstarter are that projects sent to Indiegogo receive funding as Indiegogo receives the funds, and extracts its 4.0% fee. If the funding falls short, the entrepreneur has the choice of returning it or keeping it. If the latter, Indiegogo charges a 9.0% fee.

An estimated 15 million people visit Indiegogo each month and more than 250,000 projects have been funded thus far. Projects that have received funding include the Tesla museum ($1.3 million), Stick-N-Find, a Bluetooth powered ultra small location sticker, which raised $861,165 and Let's Give Karen the Bus Monitor a vacation, which raised $703,833.

The five largest contribution raises through Indiegogo have been the following:

- Flow Hive, a honey producer, raised $12.2 million from 36,653 backers
- Sondors Electric Bike, created by Storm Sondors, raised $5.9 million from 14,645 people
- Restore King Chapel Now, by Elise Durham, raised $5.0 million from 282 backers
- An Hour of Code for Every Student, by Code.org, raised $5.0 million from 2,801 people
- Super Troopers, from Broken Lizard Industries, raised $4.5 million from 52,532 backers

Indiegogo prefers that you receive funding through your PayPal account. They have set rules such as entrepreneurs must not offer any financial incentives to backers; and entrepreneurs must not pitch any projects involving alcohol, drugs, weapons, ammunition, lotteries or gambling. And, it will not promote opportunities associated with hate, injury, death, damage to property or anything that can be distributed that violates another person's rights.

Online Funding Involving the Sale of Stock:

There is a plethora of online funding Web sites, in which the entrepreneur will be selling stock to both accredited and unaccredited investors, which are listed as follows, and described shortly thereafter:

SeedInvest.com: Ryan Felt and James Han founded this New York City online seed capital investor in 2011 and launched in 2013. It added to its own capital with a $4.15 million venture capital raise from Scout Capital and others in April, 2014. The two founders advised both the Securities and Exchange Commission and the U.S. Congress on what became the JOBS Act. Ryan and James have attracted 17,181 accredited investors to their crowdfunding business. Aspirant entrepreneurs should know that SeedInvest does a thorough vetting of applicants for capital. If the target funding size is not met, the funds are returned to the investors. SeedInvest charges a 7.5% closing fee and between $3,000 and $5,000 to manage the escrow accounts

Happy clients include Atlas Wearables ($1.4 million raised), Snapcard ($1.5 million raised), Virtuix ($3.0 million raised), Vengo Labs ($2.0 million raised) and Knightscope ($1.5 million raised). Having done well as an early stockholder in ActMedia, I love the VengoLabs story. Think of a digital, in the wall, consumer facing device that advertises products and dispenses them. It can hold up to 40 products and occupies only two feet of wall space. Every product costs $10.00 or less.

Knightscope is impressive, if the product works. The product, which looks like R-2 D-2, is a five feet tall, 300 pound rolling robot that is able to detect crimes before they happen with a variety of sensors, including video, thermal imaging, a laser range finder, air quality sensors and a microphone. And, here's where it gets interesting: the robot can do big data analytics, such as capturing license plates, suspicious looking people, facial recognition software and people's movements. It can alert law enforcement when the facts line up. The product is in Beta. When it works, it will be sold or leased to schools, shopping malls, office buildings, parks and medical facilities. Bill Lee, founder and Chief Executive Officer of Knightscope, had a 22-year history of building tech companies, and Knightscope is based in Mountain View, CA; however, Mr. Lee went to a New York crowdfunding source for launch capital. Go figure.

Texas Throws Open its Doors to Unaccredited Investors:
In response to the JOBS Act, the Texas State Securities Board, chaired by Beth Ann Blackwood, threw open the doors to the little guy, the unaccredited investor. As of February 12, 2015 Texas residents can invest up to $5,000 in start-ups, preferably in Texas, but that is not required. Four crowdfunding companies immediately responded: DreamsFunded.com, TexasCrowdFunding.com, TexasTruCrowd.com and CrudeFunders, LLC. The latter only funds oil and gas projects and the first one that it funded raised $950,000 from small investors for a well project in Ozona, TX, according to David Taylor, CrudeFunders' founder and CEO. Only one of the four listed its finders' fee, and that was Vincent Petrescu, founder and CEO of TexasTruCrowd.com. It chargers a 7.0% finders' fee. The Texas equity-oriented crowd funding companies are DreamsFunded.com and TexasCrowdfunding.com

Taltopia, LLC raises $840,000 at Go4Funding.com:
In February, 2008 Allen Vartazarian and Anthony Zanontian, recognized a large need: casting calls for artists everywhere. Theatrical productions, orchestra events, TV shows, movies and commercials are searching for actors and actors are seeking work. As Dustin Hoffman said when he won his first Oscar, "There are thousands of waiters, waitresses and taxi drivers who are as good at acting as I am. I'm just luckier, I guess, than they are." They formed Taltopia, LLC where actors, musicians, artists and other performers obtain their personal page and list their skills, their most recent work and site their 'Fan Clubs'. Industry professionals seeking to recruit talent post casting jobs and notices; and matches are made. $840,000 of equity funding was provided by members of the online crowdfunding site, www.go4funding.com.

Other entrepreneurial ventures funded by go4funding.com include TAPS, LLC and Blockheadtv.com among others. And, as I write this chapter, the following projects are listed on go4funding.com: $5.25 million for a regional Nigerian airline; a Maldives style hotel to be erected on 1.5 miles of beachfront in Java, Indonesia; a female vigilante "thriller" seeking completion funding; and a property maintenance/handyman services company in Tampa, FL.

Go4funding charges a finder's fee and for additional revenues, it welcomes advertising from, you guessed it, media companies such as Guitar Center, Amazon.com and Netflix among others. The headline message to wanna be movie stars is "Looking for Exposure? Build a fan club, book gigs, enter contests and get the exposure you deserve!"

Specialty Crowd Funders:

Starting a custom brewery or producing a craft beer; or perhaps you want to start or expand a vineyard? Send your business plan to Craftfund.com. Are you trying to buy a parcel of land, say two and one-half acres to build a building that the community needs? There is a crowd funder for that project called Ignitefunding.com. CircleUp, a crowd funder that has raised $195 million for 162 companies from accredited investors, funds retailers and consumer products companies. The Master Card Foundation Fund for Rural Prosperity has $50 million to invest in companies and projects in Sub-Saharan Africa. For healthy food projects, there are three crowd funders: Agfunder.com, Foodstart.com and Foodcrowdfunding.com.

Seedrs for International Entrepreneurs:

This international crowdfunding site was founded in 2012 as an MBA project at Oxford's Said Business School by Jeff Lynn and Carlos Silva. It raised $2,000,000 in first round funding from DFJ Spirit (an extension of Draper Fisher Jurvetson, a legendary Silicon Valley venture capital fund), AngelLabs and Digital Prophets among other angel investors. A year later, this London-based crowdfunder, raised $3,000,000 in a second round from 909 investors. The company has distinguished itself in many including raising $300,000 for the East End musical "Happy Days," raising capital from angel investors for a group of ten start-ups working with advisors at Webstart Bristol's accelerator program and selected by them; think mutual fund for start-ups. What is more, Seedrs achieved the first convertible equity security achieved in a crowd funding campaign. In September, 2014, it crowdfunded capital for a publicly-traded company, Chapel Down. And in October, 2014, Seedrs acquired Junction Investments a California-based crowd funder in order to have a platform for entering the U.S. market.

Thoughts on Crowdfunding:

Conversations with the management of many of these crowdfunding businesses lead me to conclude that they are here to stay; they are honest; they charge fees in the 4.0% to 7.5% of money raised range; and some provide advice and monitoring. I also believe the process takes about sixty days, start to finish, if your Investor Deck is acceptable to the in-take people at the crowd funders. If it needs modification, you might want to consider using Fiverr to make the necessary changes. They work for cheap and do quality work. But, that extends the fund raising period out to ninety days, or even more. Thus, it would be wise to be talking with conventional angel funds and angel clubs while working with the online crowd funding source that you selected, because with most crowd funders, you have to hit the dollar amount that you indicate or the money will be returned.

If your company is beyond start-up, and has some assets, a Jordanian peer-to-peer lender by the name of Liwwa should be given some consideration. It brings together investors seeking a current yield on their investment with entrepreneurs who prefer borrowing to selling stock in their companies. Visit liwwa.com and enjoy some very handsome reviews from satisfied borrowers.

If you are running out of money to sustain your start-up's funding effort, and if your business plan is intensely socially useful, you could conceivably go to the online personal funding sources and take-in some working capital. Several of these are Gofundme.com, Plumfund.com, Gogetfunding.com, Donationpages.com, Fundraising.myevent.com and

Unifiedforpeople.com. They charge a 5.0% fee as well. But it is worth it to keep you in the game.

Licensee Money:

The strategic alliance, if done well, is a thing of utter beauty. It generally involves a start-up company with very important technology, licensing a large company in the same or similar field to use the technology. There three kinds of licenses: make, use and sell; use and sell; and sell. Obviously, make, use and sell is more valuable to the start-up, and can command a higher upfront payment.

What are the upfront payments from the larger companies to the start-ups? There are two: an equity investment which the licensee (the large company) says to the licensor (the start-up company), "We want you to be sufficiently well-capitalized so that you can support this license you are granting to us. How would $1,000,000 for a 10.0% ownership of your company sound to you?" I call this a "Bear Hug" investment, because it is intended to keep the little company moving forward and thriving rather than the for the larger company score a huge return on investment. The licensee is saying, "We want you to be financially sound so that you can focus on new product development and upgrades, and, of course, we want you to share those with us.

What other terms and conditions come with that $1,000,000 investment?

1. We appreciate that you are able to innovate new and useful products, and bring them to market more efficiently, less expensively, and faster than we can by an order of magnitude.
2. We want to be kept informed, just as any stockholder is entitled to, about your financial health, budgets, plans – and if any of our competitors have gotten their noses under your tents.
3. We do not want you talking to any of our competitors about your innovative products or your plans. We want your complete attentiveness. (In the event the start-up has granted the large company a territorial license and not a ubiquitous license, the

start-up company is legally able to sell a license to other large companies.)
4. We may want to acquire you some day, and, by paying a little bit for some of your stock today, we could lower our overall acquisition price later on.

The Second Payment: The investment by the larger company is separate and apart from the second payment, which is part of the licensing agreement. If you are receiving one and not two payments from the larger company in a licensing negotiation, you are leaving some money on the table. Allow me to structure the negotiation for you, with the second payment described in item #6 below. Following then, are the key terms for the start-up company to set out for the larger company. In any negotiation, the side that sets the terms has a negotiating advantage. Here are your key negotiating terms:

1. Proscribe the geographic market or the vertical market in which the licensee can sell the product.
2. Is the license to make, use and sell, or just to sell (with the entrepreneurial company keeping the right to make the product and sell it to the licensee)? Try to hold onto the right to produce the product, because that gives you a second revenue channel – one is royalty payments for the license and two is sale of the product that you are licensing the use of.
3. Set a precise time period for the term of the license, such as five years.
4. Set exact minimum annual royalties. For example, 5.0% of all sales made by the larger company for a period of five years, payable to the licensor within sixty days of the end of each quarter or half year.
5. Demand and receive a right to audit the licensee's books and records to make sure the royalties paid to you are accurate. The language in the right of audit section of the licensing agreement should specify which side pays for the audit and under what conditions. For instance, if the smaller company has been short-changed by the larger company, according to the audit, the larger

company pays the auditor. If the smaller company has been overpaid by the larger company, according to the audit, the smaller company has to pay the auditor.
6. Demand an upfront payment equal to one-half of the licensee's estimated first-year royalty payments to the entrepreneurial company. The logic for this it that it is awfully expensive to audit the licensee; so, to avoid disputes at the back-end, you the larger company, need to show good faith upfront.
7. Set minimum sales targets on which royalties are based, and have the licensee agree to pay the entrepreneurial company the minimum each year (or half-year or quarter-year), whether the licensee actually makes the sales or not. This is super critical and I will explain why in a moment.
8. Clearly delineate events of default. Set these out in writing, and take back the license if the licensee defaults. For instance, are you going to permit the larger company to place its logo on your product? If the licensee receives complaints from users, which party must correct the problem? Does the licensee automatically receive product upgrades and innovations, or does that require a new license? The devils are in the details. And remember the late Andrew Grove's mission statement, *"Only the Paranoid Survive,"* which is also the name of his important management book.
9. As consideration, the entrepreneurial company may have to grant a right of first refusal to the licensee on any and all new or related products, share related research and development data, and agree to other restrictions on freedom to deal with others.

As a young associate at Kuhn, Loeb & Co., assigned to all incoming technology entrepreneurs who could find us – we didn't even have business cards, that's how difficult it was to find Kuhn, Loeb & Co. If you didn't have someone to shoe horn you into our esteemed investment bank, you couldn't get in the door – a young entrepreneur by the name of Charles Morchand came to us with a plan to send signals on the unused portion of television signals.

Television was first successfully demonstrated in San Francisco on Sept. 7, 1927. The system was designed by Philo Taylor Farnsworth, a 21-year-old inventor who had lived in a house without electricity until he was 14. While still in high school, Farnsworth had begun to conceive of a system that could capture moving images in a form that could be coded onto radio waves and then transformed back into a picture on a screen. The idea came to him while driving a tractor up and back, making rows, some of them that carried the signal and some of them empty. Farnsworth filed patents properly, but was negotiated out of them in the 1940's by David Sarnoff, a Belarus immigrant who is largely credited with inventing television. Sarnoff formed Radio Corporation of America and NBC. Among his genius strokes was popularizing radio by having the Jack Dempsey versus George Carpentier boxing match in July, 21 where 300,000 people tuned in to the fight.

To raise capital for Morchand's technology, back in 1965, we contacted RCA Corporation and licensed them the use of the ability for people to communicate with one another via the unused portion of the television signal. Morchand received a check for $25,000; and RCA Corporation put the license into a file cabinet and never commercialized it. We ate crow.

<u>Which Industries are Ripe for Licensing:</u> The industries that are ripe for disruption are those that are ripe for licensing. We know that the automobile industry is witnessing its dealer networks being disrupted by Tesla and its factories being disrupted by driverless cars. That is a very ripe industry. But, the others include the utility industry, where entire buildings, servers, coolers and routers will soon be powered entirely and solely from nearby 200MW wind farms. Reid Hoffman, the founder of LinkedIn, believes that universities will join networks in which all forms of teaching are shared. The life insurance industry is so non-transparent, that surely it will be disrupted by a completely honest online system, in which improvements in one's health through exercise and diet lowers her premiums. Gerhard Schmitt, professor of information architecture at ETH Zurich, and leader of the ETH Future Cities Laboratory in Singapore, sees a disruption of cities. He writes, "Our cities need to be responsive – this is

a more human-focused approach, where citizens can give feedback on the functioning of the city to those who run it."

The brilliant writer and thinker Stewart Brand, author of the *"Whole Earth Catalog,"* among others, described a useful way to think about change in his 1999 book, *"The Clock of the Long Now,"* to wit: Imagine a set of concentric circles, faster-moving things on the outside, slower things at the center. The surface layer represents fashion and trends, changing all the time. Then, as you move inwards, you get commerce, then slower again, infrastructure and governance, then more glacially, culture and right in the center, and the slow moving constant – nature. Think of Google's self-driving cars which appear to be safer than a human driver; but now have to deal with the slow layers of governance and culture. We don't have good means for legislation to keep up with technology.

Large corporations that have recently formed venture capital subsidiaries are indicative of their need to see innovation in order to perhaps capture it. Several of these include Wipro, the huge Indian IT staffing and software company; First Data Corp., whose customer base includes 6 million merchants that process roughly half of all credit and debit card transactions; McKesson Corp., a wholesale distributor of pharmaceuticals and medical supplies; and Santander Group, the largest bank holding company in the Eurozone. If you listen carefully, you can hear the footsteps of entrepreneurs bent on disrupting IT staffing, payment processing, drug distribution and consumer finance.

Vendor Money:

I am a firm believer on creating the "community effect" when you launch a new company. To do this, you take out a piece of paper and a pencil and write down the names of every member of your "community support team." These include vendors of products and services to your company; think law firm; think insurance agency; think temporary help agency; think local graphic design and marketing firms (to create flyers, brochures and "leave behinds"); and the local economic development agency that is charged by the city or the state to bring jobs to the community. Because you have formed your start-up to solve a problem, seize an opportunity, disrupt a tired old system or show your former spouse that you're not a loser – or perhaps a combination of these objectives, you do not have the same goals as your community members, your vendors. They see your start-up as an opportunity to bring in more revenues and to create more jobs. They have a more selfish goal.

But, that's good. When you know a vendor's objective, you can leverage it. What does that mean? It could mean asking for discounts. Asking vendors to work for stock instead of cash. When Audible, Inc. was in start-up mode, it asked the late Robin Williams to take stock instead of cash in doing book readings. The Williams estate earned more than $32,000,000 because Robin took stock and Audible was acquired by Microsoft, Inc. at $16.00 per share. When Priceline started up, it raised capital from Delta Airlines., which later sold its shares for more than $1 billion.

<u>State funding of movies</u> is a good example of vendor financing. I live in a state where the rugged terrain works for Cowboy and Indian movies as well as movies that need to replicate the terrain of Afghanistan, such as "Lone Survivor." New Mexico's attractiveness to movie and TV series producers – think "Breaking Bad" -- from Hollywood to China has resulted in roughly 200 movies being shot here. The New Mexico credit, or reimbursement to producers, is twenty-five (25.0%) percent of the "New Mexico spend." That means the dollars spent "below the line," which means for skilled people and extras who live and work in New Mexico. This typically excludes the actors and directors, because they fly in from other states. A few stars live in New Mexico including Julia Roberts and Alan Arkin.

When producers come to my office to seek funding, I calculate the New Mexico spend and contact companies that provide loans against 25.0% of that number. The most efficient of these lenders that I have found is 3point Capital.

Some states have copied New Mexico and if fact have topped it. Since New Mexico does not advance its credit upfront on the first day of filming, it has lost movies and TV series to Mississippi whose credit is 30.0%, at the time of this writing, and it advances the entire amount upfront. This has lured some films from Louisiana, whose credit is 25.0%, payable at the end of shooting.

When my investment bank was raising early-stage capital for Accentra Corp., a New Jersey start-up run by a first-time entrepreneur from New Jersey, to launch the Paper Pro Stapler, we were not finding many takers. The uniqueness of this stapler is that with a tiny touch of the finger, the staple goes through 20 pages. However, at the time Office Depot, Office Max and Staples, didn't have any incentive to offer customers anything new in the stapler category, as their Swingline and Bostitch products were moving pretty nicely. After all, all offices need staplers. If you were a fan of the movie "Office Space" you may recall the seriousness of the offence of Bill Lundburgh taking Milton's red Swingline stapler. Milton set out for revenge. When you have invented a "gotta have" product, like a stapler, and it will create *agida* for the installed vendors of that product, be prepared for a battle.

In our case, we called on a distributor who knew the buyers at Office Depot, Office Max and Staples, and the distributor convinced them to create shelf space and J-hooks to display the Paper Pro Stapler. When the distributor's CEO told the entrepreneur and me, the distributor put up the capital to launch the business.

Purchase Order Financing:

This is one of my favorite forms of financing, I suppose because it saves equity for my clients. Here's how it works. Let's say that your early stage company makes a product, and we'll say it is commercial refrigeration cases for supermarkets. If you have purchased orange juice, ice cream, milk or cheese, it is stored in these coolers or freezers. Your product is doing well, even though your company is young and under-financed.

Let's say your manufacturer is in Japan and your customers are in cities throughout the United States. Let's also that you pay $10,000 per unit and that you sell them for $30,000. Venture capitalists and small business investment companies have shunned your company, because it has cost of goods sold, or COGs, and these investors love "No COGs" companies, such as software makers, and of course, they prefer software makers that sell on a recurring revenue model, call SaaS, or software as a service. You're not stuck.

Purchase order financing companies pay for the goods to be manufactured and when they reach the dock in Japan, ready for a ship to bring them to the port in Long Beach, CA or Port Elizabeth, NJ, an accounts receivable lender pays them back, plus interest and finances the customers whom you have designated. Here's the math. Your company has orders for 30 of these cases, or $10,000 times 30 = $300,000. The purchase order financing company sends a wire transfer to the manufacturer of 80.0% of that amount or $240,000. You raise the balance on multiple credit cards or crowd funding a loan at OnDeck Capital. You find the $60,000 somewhere.

The goods are made and delivered to the dock for pickup by a ship headed for the U.S. An accounts receivable lender has credit checked the 30 customers that have ordered the cases, and they are fine with all of them. The purchase price in total is 30 times $30,000 or $900,000. The accounts receivable lender loans you 80.0% of $900,000, or $720,000. You wire $240,000 plus $10,000 of interest to the purchase order financing source, and the balance of $470,000 is your profit on the transaction. Payments are made to workers, a commission to your sales staff, rent, electricity, marketing, insurance and other bills are paid, and you have a cushion of $300,000 in the bank. All of this without any equity give-up to an angel or venture capitalist. The vendor must have good credit, must be honest and must live in a country with a responsible judiciary. If the vendor is in a country without a respected judiciary, purchase order financing will not work. Japan and Korea are acceptable and virtually any settled by the British. But, most other countries do not have non-bribable judiciaries. Purchase order financing works if the vendor is in the United States or Canada, of course.

Venture Capital Funds With Seed Capital Divisions:

As I have written elsewhere, the modern, institutional venture capital industry is fifty years old. It started in four places: Boston with American Research and Development, the first Small Business Investment Company; New York City, with VenRock, the Rockefeller Brothers' venture capital fund, Bessemer Venture Partners, the Phipps' family's venture capital fund and Whitney Ventures, the Whitney family's venture capital fund; Chicago with Heizer Capital Corp.; and Palo Alto, California with Arthur Rock and Davis & Rock, plus Eugene Kleiner's and Tom Perkins' venture capital fund and that of Hambrecht & Quist. The advent of the semiconductor and the computer made fortunes for the early venture capital funds and small business investment companies. The standard ownership structure in the early days was that labor received 20.0% of the capital gains and capital received 80.0% of the capital gains, and labor ate all of the losses. Later on, capital shared in the losses. Labor charged capital a 2.0% management fee. Thus, if your venture capital fund was $25,000,000, the management fee was $500,000, enough to pay a few people to work there.

Kleiner Perkins' third venture capital fund was $350 million in size and all of its investments were flat-out losers, save one. The one winner was Google. And, it is that kind of dice roll luck that makes venture capital investing so much fun and has attracted more than 2,200 copy cats.

When a portfolio fund IPOs (has an "initial public offering"), the venture capital fund employees who backed it usually have to wait six months – called the lock-up period – before they can sell their shares. Google IPOed at $85.00 per share. I don't know what Kleiner Perkins paid for its shares, but let's assume $1.00. The fund's managers were probably getting calls from the insurance underwriters and pension funds that back Kleiner Perkins to "sell, baby, sell." But, they couldn't. There was a lock-up period. During that lock-up period, Google's stock price nearly doubled to $150.00 per share. Thus, all the early stockholders benefited by being forced to wait.

However, times have changed. Today, there are so many venture capital funds competing for the next Google, that they are forced to go further to the earliest curve of the S-curve that you saw back in Figure 6. This means that venture capitalists have to take on more risk, and it is called "seed capital" investing

Plus, there is crowd funding, strategic investor funding, angel capital funds and angel groups and several wealthy entrepreneurs are capable of writing some sizeable checks. Adam D'Angelo, Facebook's first algorithm writer, is a human venture capital investing machine with some of his billions. He advised the founders of Instagram on technical issues and then wrote a $12,000,000 check for them, which paid him back handsomely when Facebook bought Instagram for $2 billion a couple of years later. A venture capital fund was thus deprived of that opportunity. All the more reason for venture capital funds to move out the risk curve. Grab your seat belt, is my advice, because inevitably, by taking on more risk, venture capitalists will have more losses, and there will be a decline in their number. A weeding out.

A word of advice on applying to the Seed Division of venture capital funds is do not expect a Silicon Valley venture capital fund to give your new company the time of day, unless it is populated with managers from a previous start-up that made them money. They are very insular people, and respect entrepreneurs with whom they have a prior track record. Thus warned, here are some names and Web sites from the current list provided by http://cbinsights/venture-capital-database.com.

Table 4: *SOME SEED DIVISIONS OF VENTURE CAPITAL FUNDS*

Azure Capital www.azurecap.com **and Paul Ferris has done 30 start-ups**
CrunchFund www.crunchbase/organization/crunchfund.com **M. Arrington**
Cue Ball Capital www.cueball.com **Tony Tjan, located in Boston**
Forerunner Ventures www.forerunnerventures.com**, loves consumer deals**

Green Visor Capital www.greenvisorcapital.com, fintech only, Simon Yoo
Kapor Capital www.kaporcapital.com, socially useful deals, Mitch Kapor
Kima Ventures www.kimaventures.com, funds many start-ups, Xavier Niel
Launch Capital www.launchcapital.com, likes healthcare, mobile, New York
Next View Ventures www.nextviewventures.com, diverse, Boston area
Queensbridge Venture Partners www.qbvp.com, likes media, Los Angeles
Social Starts www.socialstarts.com active investor in the social construct, NYC
Upfront Ventures www.upfront.com likes media, Los Angeles, Mark Suster

I recommend that you Google "seed capital funds" and create the list of about 50 seed funds from which I pulled off these dozen. I tried to show you diversity of location, industries of interest and whether or not they like consumer deals, tech deals or socially useful deals. Your pitch book or investor deck should be not more than 10 pages and describe the problem you intend to solve, the solution to the problem and how you intend to convey the solution to the problem; and of course, the revenue channels.

Strategic Funding Sources:

My second book, self-published in 1976, produced by me on an Olivetti non-electric typewriter and sold at a price of $65.00 was entitled *"Corporate Venture Capital Investing."* I brought in about $6,500, pretty big money at the time. It was roughly the salary of young associates in small business investment companies at the time. 1976 was a very good year for me, as the ActMedia closing fee was high five figures and other deals were closing as well.

I need to take a moment to explain that the concept of entrepreneurship as a chosen profession, in the category of lawyer, physician, accountant, engineer or teacher, had nowhere near the stature that it enjoys today. It had no stature at all. Thus, I was pioneering with books such as *"The Radical New Road to Wealth,"* published by a small Long Island firm and *"The Entrepreneurial Life: How to Go for it and Get It"* published in 1982 by John Wiley & Sons, Inc. The idea that large corporations would launch venture capital investing divisions was so disruptive and new, that I could not get a publishing house to underwrite it. I was pioneering, and pioneers often end up face down in the mud with arrows in their back. But, that wasn't my ending. I got on the phone and made 100 sales of *"Corporate Venture Capital Investing"* and although not a lot of money, I became well-known to the corporate venture capitalists and closed some deals with them.

The point I made in the book that I marketed to business development officers of Fortune's 500 largest companies was there are some very good reasons for your corporation to make venture capital investments. Only one corporate venture capital business was in operation in 1976, and that was Exxon's. Today, Intel Capital is the largest venture capitalist in the world, with 2,400 companies in its portfolio.

Typically, a corporate venture capital operation will only invest if there is a traditional venture capital fund in the deal as well. This is typically because the corporate venture capital operation does not have monitoring capability. This is not necessarily true in the life sciences market where, say an Amgen, invests in a company seeking therapies for a disease that Amgen is interested in. It is likely that Amgen will have invested with a licensing agreement, as discussed earlier in the section on licensing; because, its goal would not be capital gain, but rather having an innovative therapy to fight a disease of interest to them.

The reasons that I listed in 1976 that induced corporations to invest in early stage companies are still valid today. My staff and I interviewed all of the senior managers of the small, but active group of corporate venture capital subsidiaries. They are the following:

THE OBJECTIVES OF CORPORATE VENTURE CAPITAL INVESTING

1. To incubate and reduce the cost of acquisitions;

2. To gain exposure to possible new products for their products;
3. To add new products to existing distribution channels;
4. To expose middle management to entrepreneurship;
5. To reduce the cost of research and development;
6. To obtain a training area for bright young management trainees;
7. To utilize excess manufacturing capacity, space or personnel;
8. To mesh the activities of several departments in joint efforts;
9. To generate capital gains;
10. To "look out the window" for upcoming breakthroughs;
11. To generate income through well-conceived strategic partnerships;
12. To provide excellent group therapy for senior management;
13. To create good public relations; create lively press releases;
14. To keep pace with the competition who are probably doing it;
15. The "ITEK" reason; and
16. To encourage new company formation in the headquarters community.

Some of these reasons for investing in early stage companies need elaboration. First of all, entrepreneurs can move faster than corporate employees, and this includes the areas of research and development, new product development, scaling a business and making useful, bolt-on acquisitions. Large corporations are not able to hold onto employees with an entrepreneurial streak, and the only way to capture their zeitgeist is to invest in them. Intel Corporation has made more than 800 venture capital investments, and perhaps that is how it has achieved its reputations as one of the world's smartest companies.

The corporate venture capital managers provided my team and me these reasons, and when we asked about some of the oddest answers, such as "to provide excellent group therapy for senior management," the answer came back, thus: "Board meetings can become boring, and when that happens, the Chairman starts to tick off a few of the more exciting venture capital investments."

The "ITEK" reason stands for "I took Eastman Kodak," and came about when the research and development team within Kodak begged Kodak to invest in their new business idea. But, Kodak management refused to do so which resulted in the team leaving and founding ITEK. It grew to become a very successful business, while Kodak lost the battle for cameras by not going digital when the footsteps were clearly loud enough to be heard all over Rochester, NY and ended up in Chapter 11.

If large corporations could innovate with the speed and efficiency, and pinpoint their markets' needs as well as entrepreneurial companies, there would be no need for their entering into strategic alliances or making venture capital investments.

Some large corporations do the same thing over and over again, year after year and one wonders when they will wake up and smell the roses. Phoenix Brands, the producers of Ajax and Fab, recently filed for Chapter 11 protection, because it could not match the kind of shelf space Procter & Gamble can obtain, with its broader product line. Speaking of P&G, their Gillette division has lost significant market share to the Dollar Shave Club and Harry's Shave Club which have collectively captured more than seven million users, forcing Gillette to copy them.

I recommend your keeping a sharp eye out for large corporations that have been doing the same thing over and over again without meaningful changes in their business model. These companies may not have any terrific ideas for new products or new revenue channels, and would welcome your knock on their door. When I think about Fandango, I ask myself, "Where can they go from here?" They seem ready to pop for a new direction.

Grants and 501-C3 Buddy Cars:
There are thousands of potential grants available to entrepreneurial companies, and to attract a few hundred thousand dollars from one of them, it will likely require you hiring a grant writer to write the reasons your company is solving the kind of problem that foundations and philanthropists choose to fund. Education attracts grants like mosquitoes at an August picnic. Developing a mobile app to help managers operate

more efficiently could not bring a single mosquito to that picnic. Life sciences companies are able to attract grants relatively easily as are cleantech, agtech and enertech companies.

Grant money should always be part of an overall upfront financing plan, and not the sole or central element of a financing plan. Here is an example of how to bring grant money into your company. Let's say you have conceived of an engineering solution such as ripping up sidewalks and replacing them with sheets of steel that turn gears when people walk on the sidewalks and the gears turn flywheels, which flip on a switch to activate the HVAC system on high outdoor temperature days and lower the HVAC system on cool days. Power from the people! And power to the people in the buildings that occupy the streets. This could be called an "enertech company," which are among the most favored of investments as this book goes to press, with very large carbon emission reduction features. The test equipment and related parts could be financed with equipment loans, subject to an underpinning of angel capital. Let's say that combination is $1,000,000 of debt and $2,000,000 of angel capital, sufficient to pay the research and development team their salaries for 18 months. Now, the icing on the cake could be a $500,000 grant to be used for pure research.

A 501-C3 corporation or limited liability company would necessarily have to be created, into which the $500,000 grant financing would flow. Your accountant or bookkeeper should control the check book to make sure that no more than 10% of the $500,000 flows into the company's checkbook. That would be for purposes of the company managing the 501-C3, and for no more than that. The rest of the $450,000 must be used for research, development, testing and bringing in regulators to see the test results.

Grant proposals are similar to memoranda seeking private funding, but they stress the social utility of the project rather than the capital gain aspects. For example, a company in Western Pennsylvania that provides information technology staffers to fill needs in corporate IT departments, could create a mentoring program in a sidecar company, for the purpose of training laid-off steelworkers to become coders, and software programmers. The dual purpose is obtaining more staffers from the community, rather than bringing in H1-B workers from India or other countries, filling the need for more trained IT staffers for the needs of the community and doing well by doing good, as the expression goes. This is precisely the kind of activity for which quite a bit of grant money is available. The Kellogg Foundation and the Walmart Foundation prefer education opportunities such as this as the target of their grants.

If in the process of creating something in the not-for-profit buddy car a saleable product is created, it belongs in and must stay with the 501C-3. However, the 501 C-3 can license it to the mother ship, and the mother ship can begin selling it and paying royalties to the sidecar not-for-profit company. With those royalties, the 501C-3 can train more laid-off workers from the local steel mills and factories of Western Pennsylvania.

Research and Development Grants:
The granddaddy of all grantors is the National Science Foundation, which disburses roughly $7.5 billion each year, principally to universities for their research. However, it receives approximately 50,000 applications from small businesses each year and funds approximately 11,000 of them. The first award to a small business is $25,000 and the small business can apply again and again as it completes milestones, and the size of the grants grow to a maximum of $500,000 to any single small business. The recipients of NSF grants must be striving toward products or service of great social utility. The first proposal is to prove the concept, and the grant for that is $25,000, if the small business' proposal is accepted. And if the concept is proven, the next step up the latter is to produce a product and test its utility, for which the grant can be $125,000 or more, if accepted by the judges at the NSF. Finally, testing demand for the product can win a grant of up to $500,000. If I am making this sound too simple, there is actually not very much complexity in dealing with the NSF. It is by far and away the greatest angel funding source every conceived by any government, and Americans are fortunate that it is a 60-year-old American institution and still kicking. More companies have achieved public markets for their shares on the New York Stock

Exchange, the American Stock Exchange and NASDAQ after having received NSF funding, than from any other angel group, angel fund, venture capital fund or Small Business Investment Corporation. It is truly an American institution as great as any that man has every created. For more details on how to apply for an NSF grant, see www.nsf.gov.

Education Grants:

There are hundreds of foundations and family offices writing checks for education. For the most part, they cite specific locations for which they will provide grants. For example, the Walmart Foundation will provide $5,000 for a not-for-profit with a compelling story concerning education in a town in which they have a store. Here are some other grantors in the field of education, pulled off of the Web:

- Dub and Murray Martin Cherokee and Clay County Trust: Grants are made to organizations in Cherokee or Clay County, North Carolina that promote education programs, support and maintain churches, provide housing to the elderly, maintain children's homes or orphanages, offer financial assistance to individuals in need, care for individuals burdened with diseases, and help victims of domestic violence.
- The Cleon W. Mauldin Foundation: Grants are restricted to the Central Savannah River Area of George and South Carolina and are primarily focused on the arts (particularly music, dance, and ballet) as well as education in these fields.
- The Nunnally Foundation: The Foundation has a practice of primarily supporting charitable organizations located in the Greater Richmond, VA area. Preference may be given to programs related to healthcare, education, human services, religion, arts and culture.
- The Robert Stewart and Helen Pfeiffer Odell Fund: The Fund has a practice of making grants primarily for education and programs that support at risk youth and their families in the San Francisco Bay Area.

- Caroline J.S. Sanders Trust 1: Limited to 501 c-3 organizations, primarily located in Pennsylvania, which support education, social welfare programs, and training and education of the handicapped.

The Web provides the mailing addresses of these and thousands of foundations, the majority of which ask to receive proposals in double-spaced text, from five to 25 pages.

Searching for the Most Relevant Foundation:

Another form of search for the most likely grantors is by industry. For example, if your business is tech-oriented, you can type into Google, "Intel Foundation," the philanthropic organization owned by Intel Corporation. Voila, you virtually meet Ms. Wendy Hawkins, Executive Director, Intel Foundation, 2200 Mission College Blvd., Santa Clara, CA 95054-1549.

Or if your business is in the auto industry, type into Bing, "Ford Motor Company Foundation, and eureka, the virtually meet Mr. Jim Vella, President, Ford Motor Company Fund and Community Services, 1 American Rd, P.O. Box 1899, Dearborn, MI 48126-2798.

Perhaps, you are in drug discovery or other sections of the life sciences industry, using the same search method you arrive at Ms. Anneka Norgren, Executive Director, The Pfizer Foundation, 235 E. 42nd St., New York, NY 10017 – 5703.

Upfront financing in the digital age has been made considerably easier by the depth of data collection by Google, Yahoo and Bing. The key to bringing back the correct answer to your search questions most of the time, is to try to think like a Google, Yahoo or Bing programmer and discover the form of your question that they want you to use to bring back the best answers. Frustration should not hold you back; keep rearranging your search phrase, until "bingo" you have done it the exact way the search engine programmers wanted you to.

Case History of Melding Grants with Other Sources of Funding:

Vertical Harvest, founded by Penny McBride and Nona Yehia, who met at a party eight years ago, builds hydroponic greenhouses in which the plants, such as lettuce are grown vertically in order to capture maximum light. Vertical Harvest ships fully organic lettuce and other produce to local restaurants, grocery stores and supermarkets in and around Jackson, WY. Its current greenhouse occupies 4,500 sq. ft. in a downtown lot. With a new greenhouse just now going up, Vertical Harvest will soon be shipping 100,000 pounds of produce per year. It is part of a trend known as "farm to table" in which social entrepreneurial farming companies have grown 180 percent from 2006 to 2014, according to a government report.

The company employs 15 people who have conditions ranging from Down syndrome, autism, seizure disorders and spina bifida, and who share 140 hours a week under the customized employment model. The town of Jackson, WY is a part owner of the business, as are outside investors, and Ms. McBride and Ms. Yehia who have raised $3.8 million in public and private financing, as well as grants. The two women are growing produce vertically, selling 95 percent of what they produce, making a profit and hiring people with disabilities. Plus, the people of Jackson, WY and environs are eating lettuce and other produce that never saw a pesticide, an herbicide or a grain of fertilizer.

Leveraged Buyouts:

Alright, you want to be an entrepreneur; but, you haven't found a problem that needs a solution. You have seen and read the business plans of friends and friends of friends who have shown you the Goliath they aim to tackle with their slingshots; but, this has not stimulated your entrepreneurial brain.

Let's say that you live in Connecticut and drive or take the train to work five days a week in lower Manhattan. You know in your heart that a hovercraft would be the solution to traffic jams, pot holes, delays on the train and other *agida* creating issues. But, you haven't found the key to the door of whoever controls the docks in New York City; and so, the idea dies and waits for you to gain some wealth.

But, wealth is created entrepreneurially or by backing them, and you are neither. Yet, you have the characteristics of an entrepreneur. I wrote this in *"The Entrepreneurial Life: How to Go For It And Get It,"* thirty-four years ago: "The entrepreneur is someone dissatisfied with his or her career path who decides to make a mark on the world by developing and selling a product or service that will make life easier for a large number of people. The entrepreneur is single-minded, energetic, and has a mission and clear vision; he or she intends to create out of this vision a product or service in a field many have determined is important, to improve the lives of millions.

"This archetypal individual represents – to some – a contradiction. Until the time he conceived of his entrepreneurial (ad)venture, he worked fully within the scope of traditional societal values, for a corporation, perhaps, or for a laboratory or a medical school, or research center. He had been hired, he believed, for his creative potential, and was rewarded, he believed for his creative contributions. He was well satisfied.

"Lurking in the wings, however, was a foil. For although initially she trusted the that the organization valued her and rewarded her principally for her creative potential and output, and she had joined the organization in part because of its prestige, as she became more energetic and needed more latitude and funding for her department, the organization provided less support, financial and otherwise. She became dissatisfied with her working conditions and her trust in the organization faded. She begins to question her identity and her purpose in life. 'What will I do with my creativity?' 'What will I do with the rest of my life?'"

Assuming that he or she has not identified a problem to solve and the solution for that problem, the entrepreneur leaves the organization and buys a company. He has no money, so how does that happen. <u>It happens via the leveraged buyout.</u>

The leveraged buyout is the process of buying an existing, operating company by borrowing on its assets and cash flow, and repaying the loans from the seller's cash flow. It is so easy to do that an entire industry has formed with more than 3,500 participants called the private equity industry. The 2012 Republican Presidential candidate, Mitt Romney, ran a private equity fund by the name of Bain Capital. The Jordan Company, Carlisle, Blackstone, TPG, Kohlberg Kravis & Roberts are some of the better-known private equity funds. But, they did not invent the leveraged buyout. I think it was invented by men and women who desperately wanted to become entrepreneurs, but didn't find a problem that they sought to solve, or the solution to deliver to the problem.

Warren E. Buffett (Berkshire Hathaway, 1965), Dr. Henry Singleton (Teledyne, 1960), Jimmy Ling (Ling Temco Vought, 1960), Royal Little (Textron, 1954), and my mentor, the late Robert Davidoff, a Vice President of Carl Marks & Co., where I trained after leaving Kuhn Loeb & Co. Some of my early leveraged buyout clients include Ira G. Corn, Sash Spencer, F. Lee Bailey and Victor Kiam. My experience with Victor Kiam, who acquired Remington Brands, the electric shaver manufacturer in an all-debt leveraged buyout (meaning, Victor did not have to come up with any money) is worth telling.

Victor Kiam's All-Debt Purchase of Remington Brands

It's 1977, and I am a young investment banker. Victor Kiam, silver-haired and spry at fifty years at the time he called me, was President of Benrus Corp., the watchmaker. He asked me to assist him in buying Remington Brands, the electric shaver company, from Remington Rand, a diversified Bridgeport, CT, manufacturer of rifles and computers, among other heavy industrial products. Victor went on television after the purchase with a very convincing ad, "I liked the shaver so much, I bought the company." Because I determined that Remington was in a cash bind, I wrote up an offer for Remington that required them to take back a sellers note for 40 percent of the $4.2 million purchase price, leave all of the cash, accounts receivables, inventory, and equipment in the company but remove the funded debt. This left Victor and me to raise $2.5 million, plus my fee, or about $2.7 million.

I wrote a Leveraged Buyout Funding Memorandum and pitched it to the very few lenders that were doing LBOs in New York City at the time – Walter Heller, Rosenthal & Rosenthal, James Talcott (which my friend,

Joe Steinberg, subsequently acquired as the basis for Leucadia National Corp.) and Chase Manhattan Bank, where I had some friends who were in the emerging asset-based lending division. All of these lenders were in the garment district at the time, where the seeds of the first LBOs were being planted. I loved LBOs so much, I ended up writing three books on the subject which sold tens of thousands of copies.

Victor and I were up against a deadline to close with Remington, and we were edgy and jumpy as our lender at Chase ran his numbers. He would advance 80 percent against the selling company's accounts receivables, 40 percent against raw material and finished goods inventory and 25 percent against the depreciated value of Remington's equipment. He said, "Victor and David, you're about $350,000 short. I need a fungible asset of about twice that amount."

Without taking a breath, Victor said, "We'll be back in thirty minutes." He leaped out of his seat, grabbed my arm, and said, "David, let's go."

We left the Chase branch at 39th and Seventh Ave., hailed a taxi and drove to Murray Hill, about six blocks away on 36th Street. As we hopped out of the taxi, Victor told the driver to keep the meter running, and we bounded up the steps into his door-manned building. We took the elevator to the seventh floor, got out, and entered the Kiam residence. Victor removed his shoes and told me to do the same, and he and I stepped onto what looked like a Pierre Deux fabriced sofa, from where we carefully removed an expensively-framed painting. I believe it was an Andre Derain, an important Fauvist. We took the taxi back to Chase, and Victor and I carried the painting over to the desk where our lender was waiting.

"Here is the additional collateral you need," said Victor breathlessly. The lender looked at the painting, and Victor turned it around to show the provenance, the several galleries that had owned it and a recent appraisal that he had had done. After a couple of minutes, the lender said, "This will do the trick. You've got your loan, Victor."

How Victor explained the empty space on the wall to his wife, Ellen, a strong businesswoman in her own right, I do not know. He went on to achieve a great success with Remington, but then overextended himself with an $84 million leveraged buyout of the New England Patriots in 1988. The old Foxboro stadium did not come with the purchase, and Victor called me, actually in tears, when he needed to buy it in 1990 and renovate the bathrooms and the leaky ceilings throughout the stadium. By the time I could wrap my brain around a workout and turn around, Victor lost the stadium to Robert Kraft and shortly thereafter, lost his majority interest in the Patriots to his lender. My dear friend Victor died much too early – at age 74 in 2001.

F. Lee Bailey, who is primarily known for his skills in criminal defense, asked me to assist him with recapitalizing Enstrom Helicopter Company, a $37.5 million (revenues) helicopter manufacturer which he bought in a highly-leveraged buyout from Purex Industries. When Lee successfully defended Dr. Sam Sheppard in 1954, who was charged with killing his wife, his reputation was made. Lee and I flew into Enstrom's headquarters in a twin engine Cessna in a terrible snowstorm over Lake Michigan, which I knew was going to be my undoing. *"When I had no roof, I made audacity my roof,"* quoth the Poet Laureate, Robert Pinsky. I was picking some very audacious men to raise money for. It would serve me well. But, when you are working with someone with superstar credentials defending questionable people who were attempting to save their souls through litigation, with slim odds for winning, you get sucked into the superstar's mythical strengths. We made it safely to Enstrom's runway. I did the funding, and later on Lee sold Enstrom to Victor Kiam.

Successful entrepreneurs cannot conceive of failure. Obstacles may have to be jumped, danced around, or crawled through – or maybe they'll find new paths. But obstacles will not stop them. In the words of David J. Padwa, founder of Agrigenetics Corp., the entrepreneur's attitude toward his obstacles is: "Shoot me. It doesn't matter. I'm going to do it anyway."

Although the obstacles may deter the entrepreneur and may knock him off his path and cause a variation in the business plan, they will not kill the company. New businesses die for a variety of reasons; but if the entrepreneur possesses unvarnished courage, he will succeed. If the entrepreneur possesses back-to-the-wall, street fighter instincts, he or she is way ahead of the game of survival.

One entrepreneur expressed well how many entrepreneurs respond to doom-and-gloom messages. We were driving to a difficult meeting with a very distressed banker, and the entrepreneur said, "What can the bank do to me if I don't pay them? They can't harm me physically. They can't hold my children for ransom. They can't kill me. I am worth more to them alive and operating my company than dead with no company. So, they have got to work with me. That's why I am smiling today even though my loan is in default. I will convince the bank that they must put down their guns and get out their pens and write me a new loan."

My client in 1974, Tom Kelly, founder and President of TIE/communications, tells about his summer jobs during college. It seems that Kelly took a job as a truck driver for a soft drink bottler to help pay for college, and the other drivers thought that life was too sweet for young Tom. So they tried to run him over with a truck. If you are going to climb into the ring with AT&T in 1974, you don't back down from a bunch of 200-pound truck drivers in 1958. So Kelly grabbed a bottle, broke off the bottom until the piece he held was jagged, and told his co-workers that if he got hurt they would have scars to show for it. By that afternoon, Kelly could have been elected their union representative. It takes moxie – or, as they say in Yiddish, *chutzpah* – to be an entrepreneur.

Courage is entirely consistent with the entrepreneur's penchant for making the complex simple. No matter how many people scream, "No!" The entrepreneur keeps saying, "Yes!" No matter what obstacles are placed in the entrepreneur's path, he will find a way to get around them. If the job needs doing, she will do it. When an entrepreneur proposes marriage and is rejected, he says, "Ok, I can deal with that. Now let's talk about the wedding."

Entrepreneurs become extraordinarily self-reliant. This was functional a half century ago when the new industries were somewhat simpler; that is, housing, transportation, broadcasting. Today, when many entrepreneurial solutions are technological, most entrepreneurs need partners to cover the areas at which they are weak.

Courage is visible. People can sense leadership and courage in others and they flock to those persons. One of the reasons leveraged buy-out entrepreneurs are able to turn around tired old companies is that the employees are happier working for a charismatic leader and perform well for him. They grew tired of the "woe-is-me" president and did not produce well for him.

Entrepreneurs are very much aware of the fact that they are set apart from the rest of society because of this unique quality. It is another thing that cannot be discussed openly with others, or even defended. Thus, entrepreneurs are even further misunderstood. Considered by many to have the ethics of a used shoestring salesman, the entrepreneur regards himself as walking stride for stride with Churchill. When the entrepreneur selects a book to read for pleasure, a rare occurrence at best, it is usually a biography of a great historical figure; someone with whom the entrepreneur can draw comparisons and be strengthened. It is for her like drinking a cup of courage.

Courage is the counterbalance for fear. The successful entrepreneur is not blind to the possibility of failure. On the contrary, he knows well about the forces that could lead to the collapse of the company he is building. As the late Tommy Davis, founder of Mayfield Fund and a successful venture capitalist, said, he "tunes in" the signals of doom and destruction and sets up contingency plans that will provide a soft landing. For example, when a customer's important check is "in the mail," the entrepreneur knows it is still in the checkbook. He flies to the customer's office, pretending to make a service call, and picks up the check. He picks up another order along the way. By leaving town suddenly to get the check, the entrepreneur may have aborted an important staff meeting, stood up a supplier at lunch, missed his son's Little League game. But he got the cash necessary to keep the company floating. The time-tested war cry, "Get the cash before they crash!" must have been coined by an entrepreneur.

The legendary co-founder of the LBO, Robert Davidoff, and President of CMNY Capital, and my mentor at Carl Marks, placed a lot of stock in what he called "downside reasoning." In his investigation of an investment opportunity, Davidoff kept boring in to find the entrepreneur's contingency plans. To each answer, Davidoff fired back, "Okay, but if things don't work out that neatly, then what?" The entrepreneur who did not have multiple contingency plans to protect the company's downside did not get Davidoff's investment. The inimitable private equity investor, John W. "Jay" Jordan, was trained by Davidoff with extraordinarily positive results. He founded The Jordan Company in 1983, and still runs it, will spending more and more of his time in philanthropy. The Jordan buildings at Notre Dame came from Jay.

Successful entrepreneurs treat failure as the adversary. They acknowledge it more intently than any other businessman and set up contingency plans to help avoid it if the original plans lead them too close to the edge. Their courage, neither blind nor foolish, is part of a sound, and usually successful, plan for survival.

Entrepreneurs can identify problems, or potential problems, and also solve problems creatively. The creative person is fortunate in being able to avoid displeasure and gain personal satisfaction by the mere act of creating. He has a special gift that sets him apart, for he can lift himself out of the muck and mire of everyday frustrations. But, creatively alone will not be sufficient to succeed in the competitive world of commerce.

Entrepreneurs are rarely sick. They are rarely overweight because excess weight slows them down and leads to sickness. I have never backed fat entrepreneurs. They are few and far between.

Typically, entrepreneurs don't distort the world – not many are alcoholics – and they don't participate actively in ordinary rituals, passive escapes from reality, socially acceptable outlets for hostility and aggression. That is, the typical entrepreneur does not drink, garden, go to church or synagogue regularly, play competitive sports, read fiction. He tries to recreate the world in only one way – by first focusing on reality and then improving a small portion of it through the creation of a new product or service that gives positive benefits to a large number of people. Can one ask more of a life than to be creative? The entrepreneur is indeed twice blessed.

The Wealth-Creation Machine of the Noncreative Entrepreneur

Many entrepreneurs are not creative, which by my operational definition means they are unable to identify a problem and then the solution. Yet they possess most of the other characteristics common to successful entrepreneurs. Do they become successful entrepreneurs?

When an entrepreneur possesses all of the characteristics of the trade except the problem-finder's kind of creativity, he frequently begins buying companies. This is not to imply that conglomerateurs such as Charles Bluhdorn (Viacom) or Henry Singleton (Teledyne) lacked imagination. Rather, they and others like them desperately want to build a business, but they lack an idea of a problem that requires a solution. So they buy a company and then another, and another and still others, and mold and shape the companies they buy.

Leveraged buy-out entrepreneurs, more recently renamed "private equity fund investors," have a wonderful time putting deals together, making all the pieces fit, trying to wring more profits out of old companies, selling off the losers, and spinning off winners to the public. Royal D. Little, the founder of Textron Corp. and subsequently a successful venture capitalist with Narragansett Capital Corp., put together some marvelous companies under the same roof, including Bell (helicopters), Speidel (watchbands), Talon (zippers), Scheaffer (pens), Gorham (silverware), Homelite (chainsaws), Jacobsen (mowers), and Bostitch (fasteners). The purpose of the acquisitions was to smooth the cycle of textile equipment sales picked up in Textron's first round of acquisitions.

Charles Bluhdorn seemed to acquire for Gulf + Western (now called Viacom) companies that had entertainment possibilities. These included Paramount Pictures Corp. and South Puerto Rico Sugar Corp. The latter owned a large corner of the Dominican Republic on which Bluhdorn had built a unique resort called Casa de Campo. The golf course there is comparable to Pebble Beach, take it from me.

James J. Ling built LTV Corp, through a series of acquisitions that began with Ling Electric Contractors, which he launched in 1946 by selling his house for $3000 and then selling stock from a booth at the Texas State Fair. Ling went at the deal-making business with an unusual zeal as well as a sense of humor. After acquiring Wilson Company, he split it into three separate corporations: sporting goods, pharmaceuticals, and dairy products. Then he sold 20% of each of these corporations to the public. The brokerage community detected the humor as well and nicknamed these companies "Golfball, Goofball, and Meatball." They even began a rumor that Ling was going to acquire AT&T:

> Broker One: Yeah, and then he's going to split it into three separate corporations and sell 20% of each one to the public.
>
> Broker Two: What is he going to call them?
>
> Broker One: Ding-a-Ling, Ding-a-Ling-a-Ling and Ding-a-Ling-a-Ling-a-Ling.

Ah, the early LBO guys were a riot to be around. A leveraged buy-out is the purchase of a company by borrowing on its assets and repaying the loan in the future out of its cash flow. It was relatively simple back in the 1970s for an entrepreneur to locate, investigate, negotiate for and acquire a $20 million (sales) company without investing more than $20,000 in legal, accounting, travel, and lodging costs. Most leveraged buy-out entrepreneurs became so adept at investigating, negotiating, and buying companies that they keep doing it. In this way they built conglomerates, potpourris of different companies. If there are several industry groupings among the companies they acquire, the brokers may later attempt to put a label on the company other than conglomerate. But the company is the result of one man's lust to do some one thing very well, and absent a solution to a problem he had first identified, he set about buying companies. As the venture capitalist Ed Goodman says of these men, they have "whims of iron."

Today, there are more than 3,500 private equity funds with over $7 trillion doing what Messrs. Bluhdorn, Singleton, Ling, and my clients Ira Com, Sash Spencer, and Victor Kiam did independently.

Life Before Private Equity Funds

The leveraged buy-out, contrary to popular myth, was not invented by Henry Kravis or Mitt Romney and the other *cenacles* and cliques over whom the financial media now fawn as if they were geniuses. Bloomberg talking heads genuflect when Carl Icahn stops by to give an interview, and he is pleased to be worshipped. So worshipped are these heads of private equity funds that their media kneecap suckers feel that they are *aides de camp* or honorary cong guerilla, who have parted the waters and turned water into wine. Not so. They are smart copy-cats. But, the story begins in the late 1960s and I was there doing some of the earliest leveraged buyouts of the modern era. The relevance of this is that I became adept at saving broken companies using LBO strategies, and I have saved a bunch.

There are three kinds of LBOs, and I backed an entrepreneur who did each one of them multiple times with amazing grace and the brilliant use of leverage as there were few venture capital and no private equity funds back then, just a handful of conglomerateurs. My clients for the convertible preferred stock leveraged-buyout were Ira G. Corn and Sash Spencer, and we used the models created by Charles Bluhdorn, of Gulf & Western Industries fame (now Viacom); Harold Geneen who bought ITT, Sheraton Hotels, Avis Car Rental Co., Pennsylvania Glass Sand, and many others; and Henry Singleton, the entrepreneur who built Teledyne with more than one hundred acquisitions, and one assistant, Themos Miklos.

In the convertible preferred stock model, you begin with a small publicly-traded company or you buy a public shell and put an operating company in it in order to have a near-liquid currency in addition to cash and notes with which to make acquisitions. Operating companies are brokered by sell-side merger and acquisition brokers, and there are at any one time several thousand companies for sale. They can be acquired by using classic leveraged buy-out tactics as shown momentarily. Public shells are also purchased from shell brokers and owners, and they cost relatively little depending on the strength or weakness of the initial public offering market. A robust and buoyant IPO market means that public shells are not in heavy demand and, thus, are inexpensive, perhaps $150,000 for a "clean" one - no liabilities - without cash. A weak IPO market drives up public shell prices.

Once you own 90 percent of a public shell, you can split the outstanding shares 100 for 1 or 1,000 for 1 and create 100,000,000 shares outstanding from 1,000,000 shares that once were outstanding, or you can split them back to 10,000,000 shares outstanding if there were too many shares outstanding. So, let's use 10,000,000 shares outstanding.

The price per share of your company's 10,000,000 shares is, let's say, $0.03, and the stock trades "by invitation," which is Wall Street parlance for "hardly at all." You identify your first acquisition candidate whose owner wants liquidity but is willing to accept your company's convertible preferred stock (or if he wants greater security, you can offer him a convertible debenture). Because preferred stock is a security that is senior to common stock and comes with a dividend, you propose a conversion price of $0.10 per share.

The stock price of your roller-upper company begins to trade as you announce your second acquisition. This one using a dividend-paying preferred stock that converts at $0.20 per share. The conversion price of the third acquisition is at $0.40 per share and so on until you go after larger deals using much higher conversion prices.

The dividend payments are made with the cash flows of the acquired businesses. Savings are achieved by canceling the salaries of the unnecessary owners and their nepotistic employees. Often back offices can be consolidated to achieve further savings. Cash should be building up due to these savings plus earnings growth, and the debt and preferred stock can be prepaid and paid down to reduce leverage.

In 1972-1980, when Ira G. Corn of Michigan General Corp. was my client, we bought eleven companies ranging from paperback book publishers to highway sign manufacturers. I negotiated half of them and became reasonably persuasive at inducing sellers to accept both delayed dividends and progressively higher conversion prices. Ira was a delight to work with, and his untimely death in 1980 at age 60 was a terrible blow to all of his teammates at the Dallas Aces and Michigan General.

The Math of the LBO

To assess the do-ability of an LBO with all debt, and no money out of your pocket, here are some ratios you need to know:

Borrowing on the Accounts Receivable: You can borrow roughly 80% on all accounts receivable of the seller that are under 90 days old. If there are very few over 90 days, the asset-based lender might provide a revolving line of credit of 85% of all accounts receivable under 90 days. A revolving line of credit means that when you make a new sale, say of a $1,000 product, you send the invoice to the asset-based lender, and it puts $850.00 into your account at its bank. When that invoice is collected, the bank takes it in and puts $1,000 into your account, repays the $850.00 advance, takes a few bucks for interest, and you have $147.50 or so in cash availability.

Borrowing on Inventory: If you need to borrow 90% on inventory to generate enough cash for the purchase, you will need to pay for an orderly liquidation value of the inventory, and that will set you back $7,500 to $10,000. If you can get away with a conventional loan on the seller's inventory, you can expect a 50% advance against finished goods inventory. Nothing on work in process. And, if the raw materials are fungible, like rolled steel, you can borrow 50% on their value as well.

Borrowing on inventory made in Myanmar or China can occur with what is known as Purchase Order Financing which was described above. Your asset-based lender, or a P.O. Financing source that it prefers to work with, will advance 50% of the value of the goods being produced for the seller and when those goods reach the dock in Myanmar or China, the asset-based lender writes a check to the P.O. lender for the 50% value of the goods, plus interest, and the ABL advances 80% against the value of those goods, if there are invoices to purchase them.

Borrowing on equipment of the seller: This ratio is all over the lot. I have seen it as high as 80% for machinery in superb condition making those zip-lock type of clear plastic bags that we see in grocery stores or the Dollar Store and buy them to wrap sandwiches in. But, for the most part, ABLs will only go as high as 50% on used equipment.

The cost of this money is around 4.5% to 5.25% as I write this book.

Thus, if your seller has accounts receivable of $2,500,000 and inventory of $1,500,000 plus equipment at a depreciated value of $1,000,000, you might be able to borrow a secured loan of $2,000,000 on the accounts receivable, $750,000 on the inventory and $500,000 on the equipment, for an asset-based loan of $3,250,000 created for you to buy the seller.

But, the seller wants a price of $5,750,000 cash at closing. Where does the rest of the money come from? It comes from a mezzanine lender. These are cash flow lenders. They do not seek collateral, because the role they fill in the North American economy is cash flow, unsecured, subordinated loans. They will generally loan 4.0x the trailing 12 month EBITDA, which means earnings before interest taxes, depreciation and amortization. If this particular target has EBITDA of $400,000, you could borrow as much as $1,600,000 from a mezzanine lender. This loan, added to the ABL's loan of $3,250,000 gives you $4,850,000. You are $900,000 short of the seller's requirement. Where does that come from?

It comes from two places. Most mezzanine lenders require the sellers to take back a sellers' note for some of the purchase price. Let's say the sellers are persuaded to take back a note for $500,000. These are not high-interest rate notes, usually around 6% interest. You're still $400,000 short and you don't have it to put in. Here's what you do: you tell the lender that the gentleman who has been running the company will not be there and his salary will be added to EBITDA to created Adjusted EBITDA. If he was making $200,000 a year with his perks (company credit card is typical; health insurance is also typical), then you add that to the company's EBITDA and Adj. EBITDA is now $600,000; Four times that is $2,400,000 and when added to the sellers' note of $500,000 and the ABL of $3,250,000, you come up with a total borrowing capacity of $6,150,000, which includes the fee paid to investment banks like mine, plus legal fees.

Will $600,000 in cash flow support all of those interest payments? Mezzanine loans have no monthly repayment schedule, but rather a fifth year balloon. So, $2,400,000 x 10%, means that the mezzanine lender will be paid $240,000 in the first year. $3,250,000 x 5% means that the asset-based lender will be paid $162,500 in first year interest. And the seller will be paid 6% on its $500,000 subordinated note, or $30,000. The sum of the three interest payments is $432,500. When divided into Adjusted EBITDA of the Debt Service Ratio is 1.38x. That is relatively low, but above the cut-off of 1.25x, below which lenders will ask the buyer to put in equity for 10% of the purchase price. But, if the Debt Service Ratio is above 1.25x, you can have the company that your father didn't leave you. You can be the entrepreneur who is running his own business. That's the beauty of the leveraged buyout.

Other LBO Models
Some lenders insist on the buyer putting his "butt on the table." The butt on the table money is the buyer's equity in the company he or she is buying, and it is just enough to "hurt." In a $5 million leveraged buyout, the lender may require a $100,000 personal commitment and a similar amount in a $1 million buyout. It is possible to negotiate this requirement away by using the seller's note as equity or giving a validity guarantee, i.e., agreeing not to leave if the company starts to sink, but rather to remain with a baling bucket until the company is saved or dies.

Another model of the LBO stresses seller financing. As you assemble your takeover team, you must bear in mind the need to invest something other than cash in any takeover that you are planning if you intend to leverage it with loans from asset-based lenders. You may be able to circumvent butt on the table money if you buy a local company using your traditional local bank, which has provided you with loans in the past, which you have consistently paid back. Additionally, <u>if you negotiate a buyout with seller financing, you may not have to invest any of your own money or organize an investor group</u>. Seller financing usually consists of giving the seller the company's cash and accounts receivable, then paying either a sales royalty, consulting fee, or subordinated note for the balance of the purchase price. The seller keeps as collateral the stock of his company until he is fully paid out. There may be some restrictions on the amount of senior secured debt you can put ahead of your obligation to pay the seller. When asked for the personal guarantee, offer the validity guarantee instead.

Work-in-process inventory is unacceptable because it is unfinished, incomplete, and therefore nonsalable. Salable inventory (except rental inventory) is frequently undesirable collateral because, in liquidation, borrowers can back up a few trucks and empty the plant before the lender can get there. If the lender loans against accounts receivable and finished goods plus raw material inventory, it may secure the inventory by installing in the borrower's plant a warehouse company that puts a chain link fence around the collateral and locks the door when the warehouseman leaves the premises.

Inventory that is new to the economy and has not achieved an established auction market is unacceptable as well. For example, certain lasers and new forms of medical test equipment are unacceptable to most lenders due to lack of familiarity and experience with the collateral.

Prior to preparing to visit asset-based lenders, become familiar with what is and what is not acceptable collateral. You may want the seller to keep the assets that are unacceptable collateral as part of the purchase price.

Table 5: ACCEPTABLE AND UNACCEPTABLE COLLATERAL FOR ASSET-BASED LOANS

	Acceptable		Unacceptable
Accounts Receivable	If outstanding less than 90 days and if owed by businesses rather than individuals or government agencies	Accounts Receivable	If over 90 days and if owed by individuals or government agencies including school districts, the military, and "authorities"
Inventory	Raw material and finished goods, but only if the lender has a lien on accounts receivable; certain fresh rental inventory – such as instructional DVDs and rental cars are acceptable without a lien on receivables	Inventory	Work in process and raw material that is specialized or shaped to fit into or with another component; obsolete finished goods inventory

Finding targets to acquire and then convincing them to let you borrow on their assets is a skill you will need to cultivate. I watched in awe how John W. "Jay" Jordan II did it when he was 30 years old as an associate at Carl Marks & Co. One day Bob sent Jay out into the corn fields to investigate a potential buyout candidate. He was gone three days. When he finally returned, he brought with him a signed letter of intent at a purchase price so low, even Bob blushed. "Jay was relentless in the pursuit of sellers," says Joseph S. Steinberg, another Davidoff protégé, who went on to build Leucadia National Corp., sometimes called the "Junior Berkshire Hathaway." "Jay would follow the guy to his house, play with his dogs, help him mow his lawn – Jay knows all about tractors

– and sleep in his den if that's what it took to get him to sell," said Davidoff.

After nine years at Carl Marks, Jay left to form his own private equity fund, The Jordan Company, which today has total assets of $6 billion and owns more than 90 companies which include American Safety Razor, Carmike Cinemas, Fannie May, Great American Cookie, Harvey Gulf, Lepage's Industries, Lincoln Industrial Corp., Newflo Corp., RockShox, Rockwood Industries, TAL International Group, Universal Technical Institute and many more.

Joe Steinberg's Leucadia National Corp. mean time has grown to a market capitalization of $10.6 billion and Joe's ownership is worth $700 million. Just recently, Leucadia acquired Jeffries, Inc., the mid-market investment bank whose CEO became Leucadia's CEO, bumping Joe up to Chairman. Davidoff taught his young men quite well.

The Workout and Turnaround LBO

While searching for a terrific LBO candidate, you come upon a company that is on death's doorstep. If you are of a fearless nature, I suggest you give it a good hard look. It may be that the owners are overly frightened, and do not know how to "stretch out the debt." I know how, and thus I loved doing workouts and turnarounds, because they were another form of the "chase," in many ways similar to start-ups. I cut my teeth on Mine & Smelter Supply Co., Denver, CO, an $85 million sales company founded in 1909 that was over-extended with vendors and lenders in 1979

I needed to buy time to figure out how to save Mine & Smelter. Among the techniques I found useful to buy time to compromise more than $20 million in accounts payable and funded debt was to change the voice that spoke with the creditors. Here is what I wrote about a unique means of stretching out the creditors in my 1995 book, *The Business Bible of Survival,* published by Prima Books, Inc.

You should play the role of controller and get on the telephone with creditors, who haven't been paid in three or more months, and act dumb on the telephone. Why? Because *dumb is smart.*

Here's what you tell creditors, "I don't know where anything is," or, "I just got here, and I can't find anything."

The creditors will be nonplussed. "What do you mean you can't find anything. I've been billing you turkeys for three months, for Chrissake!"

Let the tirades pour in. Let the waves break over your head. Take the insults, the slams, the curses, and the blows. After all, you did not create the debt. "I'm here to figure things out and to get you paid," you should say.

The creditors will very likely scream back, "How in the hell can you get me paid? You can't even find my invoice."

Then you respond, "Send me a new one," which will buy you another week.

As the new invoices arrive, you and your newly-installed, real controller can talk about a plan of action. You should explain how deep the crisis is, whether it has bottomed out, whether there is a way out, and whether you can see the light. Let your controller know how much longer to play dumb or when to begin thinking about a payment plan. Assume that the new controller must buy you two more weeks by playing dumb; enough time to develop payment plans for each creditor.

She returns to her stack of phone messages and begins returning calls one by one.

"Hello. This is Gabby Hayes," the controller says as he telephones the creditors.

"Who?" the creditors ask.

(For those of you who have never heard of Gabby Hayes, he was Gene Autry's sidekick in 1950s westerns. He was befuddled by complex things, and his favorite expression was "Dag nab it!" His bafflement made all of us feel a little brighter, and we laughed with relief.)

"Who the heck is this?" the creditors ask again.

"Gabby Hayes, the new controller at XYZ Diversified," says.

"Oh, for Pete's sake. I should have known." The creditors are relaxed and amused. They will accept a small crumb from the table. Here is the crumb.

"The boss is working on a plan to pay you guys. I haven't heard all the details, but I think you're going to like it."

"Is it cash? Is it a note? What is it?" they demand to know.

"Dag nab it! I don't know what it is."

"Then how do you know I'll like it?"

"Look, some guys aren't going to get as good a deal as you. The boss likes you. He needs your product (or service). All I know is that he said to mark your invoice A, and that means pay."

"When?"

"When, what?"

"When are you going to pay me?"

"I don't know. I haven't seen the plan. Let's talk tomorrow," the controller says. Then says, "Goodbye" and hangs up.

Now, the dumb stall will not work forever, nor will it work on all creditors. Creditors usually fall into three categories:

- The creditor's accounts receivable clerk
- A collection agency employee
- An attorney

The accounts receivable clerk is doing his job. Company policy will determine how much time he has to collect an account before it is written off. This period might be anywhere from 90 to 180 days, depending on a number of things such as when the creditor's fiscal year ends. The creditor's CPA firm could insist on writing off any debt over ninety days old. At this point, the debt is either sold or assigned to a collection agency.

Collection agencies such as Dun & Bradstreet are trained collectors. They are schooled in getting money out of people; it is their reason for being. However, they have time limits as well, and if they do not collect the amount owed their client within ninety days – the usual time allowed – the collectors will lose their commission or their profit.

Collectors do not know the account very well, nor do they know the historical relationship between the creditor and the customer. A clever controller can tie the collector in knots for a while by referring to possible goods shipped back, credits to the account, improper invoices, and conversations between the company and the creditor. This line of conversation is different from what the collector is trained to say. He focuses on getting a check: when he can expect it, what the check number is, how it will be sent, whether it will be certified, and what the amount is – immediacy and specifics.

Often, the collector sits in a room with other collectors, all of them facing a wall with a thermometer on it. They all have goals. The idea is to raise the level of the thermometer to a certain dollar amount by a certain date. Their bonus is greater for faster collection of larger amounts. But occasionally, collectors go beyond good business practices. A collector once called a small company and asked to speak to the president.

"Who is calling?" asked the secretary.

"Jim Smith," the collector replied.

"From what company?" the secretary asked.

"Tell him it's about his children," the collector said.

The secretary had no choice but to put the president on the telephone. When he heard it was a collection agency, he nearly tore the telephone out of the wall. A follow-up letter to the state's attorney general ended the young man's career as a collector.

Collectors will find your home telephone number and badger you in the evenings and on weekends. Their favorite line is, "I will have to turn this over to legal," which is fine. If they do not collect the amount owed within a few weeks, they will lose the collection assignment to a lawyer.

When the unpaid invoice is given to a lawyer, it is not the end of the world. The lawyer may want to run up a time sheet on the matter before he settles it. In that case, he will probably begin with a long letter in which he paints a picture of the various horrors that are likely to befall you. "The plagues of Egypt will be brought on your doorstep," the letter might suggest. "Blood will spill," it may add. "Your children will grow up to despise you," might be the final inference.

Now, in fact, as long as the creditor's lawyer does not know the other creditors or their lawyers, he cannot put the debtor into involuntary bankruptcy. Never share the creditor list with any of the creditors. Three creditors that are each owned more than $5,000 can get together and fling your company into involuntary bankruptcy. *"If your nerve deny you, go above your nerve,"* Emily Dickinson.

Working Quietly is the Best Advice I Can Give You

The way we saved failed businesses in the 1970s and 1980s, to avoid the obsequies of death, prior to the rebarbatively adipose sums of venture capital and private equity money being thrown at entrepreneurs today, was to reverse merge then into public shells or small public companies and then make acquisitions for public stock of healthy businesses, thus to borrow on the assets of the including healthy companies and to repay the debt from the healthier target companies' cash flow. I used this strategy many times with Speed Cell Wireless Corp., on which my angels and I earned 800 percent in less than a year and when our angels and I flipped our investment in the Chicago ISP, Megsinet, to Core Comm, Inc., for a 100:1 cash-on-cash return inside of two years back when ISPs were sprouting like sunflowers in an April field in Kansas.

I arranged a conventional LBO with Bustin Industrial Products, bought by MW Supply, Inc., and now part of R-O-M Corp.,

We didn't talk much about our successes back then, be they smart start-ups that paid their backers 100 to 1 or successful workouts and turnarounds that morphed into the infrastructure of public shells and were funded with the excess cash flow, after debt service of the acquired companies. My motto, drilled into me by Charles Ely, a wizened senior partner of KL back in 1967 was, "If you don't have to write it, say it. If you don't have to say it, whisper it. And if you don't have to whisper it, just nod." Gentlemen were as quiet as paper money itself back in the day.

Today, there is a whole lot of shakin' goin' on, and it is the public shaking of one's wealth. Nick Bilton, in a 2013 article in the *New York Times*, said it like this[2]:

> "The people making money from successful start-ups are spending it, too. Last month, RealtyTrac, a real estate analysis firm, reported that Silicon Valley led the United States in the number of homes sold for $1 million or more.
>
> Let's not forget the tone-deaf parties, like one for David O. Sacks, the founder of Yammer, who sold his company to Microsoft this year for $1.2 billion. He spent about $1.4 million on a 40th-birthday bash for himself. The theme was, "Let him eat cake."
>
> Mr. Sacks asked guests not to share pictures of the event on social networks. Snoop Dogg, who was hired to sing at the party, shared pictures anyway of people in 18th-century French clothes.
>
> 'Today, being a venture capitalist is more about a lifestyle than it is about investing,' said Roger McNamee, a co-founder and managing director of the

---

[2] Nick Bilton "For the Entrepreneurs of Silicon Valley, an Embarrassment of Riches." New York Times, February, 2013. *Back*

> *technology investment firm Elevation Partners. 'They're making a million bucks a year without generating much, if any, return. It's like watching Fox News – these people are living in an alternate reality.'*

> *This trend extends beyond the new fee-hungry venture capitalists. 'Just as venture capital has become a lifestyle, you now have a generation where being an entrepreneur is a lifestyle,' he said. This is evident in the ease with which 'entrepreneurs' are given millions of dollars to create companies that differ only slightly from other successful start-ups – like Instagram for video, or Twitter for cats."*

It was not like this in the mid-1960s through the early 2000s. Money to launch companies was dear. But, in today's world where angel capitalists are funding look-alike start-ups with easy money and crowd funding sites are springing up like tulip bulbs in Amsterdam, venture capitalists are writing bigger and bolder checks to establish their fading relevance. The four hot areas that venture capitalists are chasing is called "SMAC" by the inimitable Forrester research firm. "SMAC" stands for "Social, Mobile, Analytics, and Cloud." Of these, the team in my investment bank likes the analytics sector because the companies are industry-facing with software-as-a-service, or "SAAS" revenue models and low COGs.

Business is war and one of the greatest authorities on military strategies, Sun Tzu, wrote 2,000 years ago:

> *"All warfare is based on deception. A skilled general must be master of the complementary arts of simulation and dissimulation; while creating shapes to confuse and delude the enemy he conceals his true dispositions and ultimate intent. When capable he*

feigns incapacity; when near he makes it appear that he is far away; when far away that he is near."[3]

Entrepreneurs who appear competent and who surround themselves with well-known captains of industry and science and who talk about how they are going to take over a marketplace in the business press cause their enemies to load their war planes and immediately take steps to wipe them out. Some idiotic, private company CEOs give their company's annual revenue number to Inc. magazine, for all the world to see.

Business Development Corporations

Perhaps the most flexible lenders in the country are the business development corporations, or BDCs, which are chartered by the states to makes loans to small businesses. They are a pretty well-kept secret. Not many entrepreneurs know about them. And many states do not have a BDC, but the states that do include Arkansas, Georgia, Iowa, Kansas, Maine, Massachusetts, Mississippi, Montana, Nebraska, New Hampshire, North Dakota, South Carolina and Wyoming. The Wyoming BDC has been particularly active, having funded several hundred start-ups and early stage companies over the last forty years.

The "eligible" investments of BDCs include small privately-held businesses, or small publicly-held businesses with market capitalizations under $250 million, but not an investment company, has total assets of less than $4 million and net worth of net less than $2 million. BDCs may invest in either debt or equity of eligible companies. Many BDCs operate Small Business Investment Companies, which will be described shortly. Their flexibility is greater than with any other sources of funds for small businesses, to wit:

1. Like a commercial bank, they can make conventional loans, secured or unsecured.

---

[3] Sun Tzu, *The Art of War*, introductions by Samuel B. Griffin, Oxford University Press, London, 1963, p. 41. Reprinted here by permission of Oxford University Press. Back

2. They can enter into purchase/leasebacks, whereby they might buy a plan for a small company and lease it to the company.
3. They are generally lenders under the Small Business Administration 501 program, which means that they can make loans 90% guaranteed by the SBA.
4. Many BDCs own and operate Small Business Investment Companies thus permitting them to make venture capital investments and loans.
5. BDCs are frequently run by people who are active in their communities, and can pull together angel investors from the community to fund or partially fund a start-up company.

The smaller the state, the more effective the BDC, because the state typically lacks angel capital groups, venture capital and angel funds and creative lenders. In my adopted state of New Mexico, I launched an angel dinner club, and we met on the third Thursday of each month for eleven years. I moved to Santa Fe, NM in 1981 and within a few months a Los Alamos pharmacologist by the name of Gary Seawright came to the club and presented his story for 50 assembled people who I did not know, but were obviously desperate for an opportunity to make investments in start-up companies. They listened to Gary talk about his RFID chip and its many uses and backed him in what became the E-Z Pass, affixed to more than 27,000,000 cars and trucks in the U.S. and about half that in Europe; plus, affixed to every large cargo ship in the world. E-Z Pass created 164 tech jobs in Santa Fe, and then it was whisked away when Ross Perot's venture fund put in $6 million and moved the business to Plano, TX. Today, more than 18,000 people work in the two businesses that the little angel club in New Mexico helped to launch 34 years ago. That's the power of people in small states collaborating to create, fund and support problem-solving companies.

Approaching a BDC for Funding

If you have a BDC in your state, you should set up a plan to execute the collaboration plan that I did for E-Z Pass. The first visit is to the junior college or technical school in your community to determine if they are producing the kinds of graduates that could do the tasks that your business requires. I once co-founded a truss manufacturer near Albuquerque, and we became so booked with orders, we had to hire non-violent prisoners from the local prison to produce the trusses. A visit to the local banks to ask what they can do for your start-up may be a waste of time, but among other things you will want someone to watch your bank account and prevent useless fees. The bank can issue your company's top people company debit cards. Calling on the local insurance agent is important because these folks know everyone in town usually and can open doors; plus, your start-up will need property and casualty insurance and down the road, an employee health insurance plan and directors and officers liability insurance. The latter is currently very pricey, at $6,000 per million and most directors of companies want more protection than one million dollars. It is better to put these wise women and men on a Board of Advisors until your company is strong enough to afford D&O insurance.

I also recommend meeting the best real estate agent in town, or maybe two of them, because they can be of great help in locating the best place for your headquarters. And, you will need an accountant and a business lawyer. The latter must have malpractice insurance for securities work, or if he or she tries to represent you in the closing of your angel funding, he could mess things up.

After five days of meeting all the people who can help you with advice, funding, insurance, an office, an accountant and sources of funding. There may be an angel club nearby as there are 220 in the U.S., which means most states have at least one.

In the digital age, you can Google business development corporation and enter the name of your state, to see if there is one near you. The same for angel clubs.

State Funding Programs

Where you live is frequently more important in raising capital for a start-up than is the entrepreneurial opportunity that is attempting to launch. Eight hundred start-ups were funded in New York in 2015, most of them social networks or mobile apps. Northern California is the home of Silicon Valley, where hundreds of companies are funded each year. San Diego, CA attracts life sciences companies, as does Research Triangle Park in North Carolina. Nashville likes hospital management companies and software companies that service them. Massachusetts attracts brilliant entrepreneurs such as Bill Gates and Mark Zuckerberg, but has been having difficulty holding onto to them. I believe that there will be a stunning comeback in Massachusetts, with entrepreneurs flocking there as they do to San Jose, CA.

SPARO, raised $100,000 from the Maryland Technology Fund. SPARO owns some strong patents and has built the technology to enable an online retailer to encourage customers to make a donation to one of 100 different charities as they check-out. This service increases the number of people who actually check-out rather than merely fill their basket and do not check-out by more than 66%. Fortunately, Rob Sobhani, PhD, the founder and CEO of SPARO (www.sparo.com) lives in Maryland, and the Maryland Technology Commercialization Fund ("TCF") lives there two. If you visit http://tedco.md/program.com, you will learn that TCF provides up to $225,000 to support projects that advance technology toward commercialization. TCF assists companies to reach a critical milestone in their development that will move their technology further along the commercialization path, thus to increase the company's valuation for the next round of funding. TCF makes its investment in two tranches. The first one is $100,000 for critical product development. The second one, $125,000 is made alongside an investment by a qualified investor, which means an angel or a venture capital fund.

If you are starting up in the state of Ohio, you are blessed as well. Elected officials in the Buckeye state created the Ohio TechAngel Fund ("OTAF") by raising funding from 300 high net worth Ohioans. Since 2004, OTAF has invested more than $14 million in 50+ Ohio-based technology startups. The mission statement of OTAF is "...to build wealth in Ohio by helping build great companies that can rapidly scale and attract the interest of strategic acquirers within three to five years. OTAF members may invest on their own, and thus far have written more than $15 million for OTAF portfolio companies." OTAF is currently accepting funding submissions for OTAF IV, which will invest $325,000 in the high tech startups that it chooses. The Web site of OTAF is https://rev1ventures.com/investments/techangel-fund.

Another rust belt state that lost quite a few jobs when automobile manufacturing moved to Mexico and elsewhere is the Hoosier state – Indiana. But, it was not asleep at the switch and has several funding sources for home grown businesses. In January, 2016, Purdue University in West Lafayette, IN announced that it will be investing more than $250 million in life sciences startups. The money will come from a current $2 billion capital campaign. The CEO of Eli Lilly & Company, a giant pharmaceutical company located down the road in Indianapolis is pretty happy about the Purdue initiative, as it will likely have first looks at strategic investment opportunities in new therapies. The web site is https://www.purdue.edu/newsroom/releases/2016.

Pennsylvania which has lost millions of steel-related jobs over the last few decades is another state that knows that entrepreneurs create more jobs than do the powers-that-be in the South who think bringing in a Nissan or Toyota plant and waiving real estate taxes for decades is the way to go. The Ben Franklin Technology Partners Fund, based in Philadelphia, has been backing Pennsylvania entrepreneurs for 30 years. The Ben Franklin fund invests in "marketable innovations developed in our service area." And it provides mentoring and support initiatives. Its typical check size is $50,000. The web site is http://cnp.benfranklin.org.com.

The rust belt states have the best and most active startup funding programs. These are the states from Massachusetts to Wisconsin. The states that thrive on tourism – Arizona, Colorado, Florida and New Mexico – do not have terrific state funding programs.

Small Business Investment Companies

If you are a startup entrepreneur, the Small Business Investment Company ("SBIC") program does not have you in its plans. They do not fund start-ups. They do participate in leveraged buyouts and management-led buyouts very aggressively, primarily as mezzanine lenders.

The role of the mezzanine lender is to provide five-year, cash flow loans, unsecured, and with interest payments only for 60 months, and a balloon payment of the principal amount of the loan in the 60th month. The loans are generally unsecured and do not require personal guarantees. The amount that you can borrow from an SBIC to effect an LBO or a management-led buyout ("MBO") is 4.0x the Adjusted EBITDA of the target company. If you make an equity investment in the buyout, or bring in an equity investor, the mezzanine lender may go as high as 4.5x Adjusted EBITDA.

The company that you are trying to acquire may be a social media or a software as a service company which collects its subscription fees in advance, and has no accounts receivable and no inventory. In that event, you will not be able to attract an asset based loan, and you will rely exclusively on the mezzanine lender to make your buyout. Therefore, it is important that you know how to collect and calculate "add-backs".

Add-Backs

These are the expenditures of the target company that will not be there after you own the Company. The most typical add-backs are the following:

1. The owners' salaries;
2. The owners' health insurance; perhaps life insurance;
3. The owners' "perks," which is usually his and his spouse's use of a company credit card to buy gas, food, dinners, personal items and travel;
4. A nepotistic salary, for example, a brother-in-law who does relatively little and gets paid a living wage;

5. The accounting department may have too many people in it, may not be using some of the modern credit department software proffered by Intuit and others, and thus one of the people in that department may be obsolete;
6. And, finally, there may be some vestigial costs that nobody has noticed in the last few years, such as leaving the air conditioning on at night, or paying a service company a monthly fee, even when it doesn't provide services each month.
7. Remember to add back your salary, if you intend to run the company post-acquisition.

If you intend to buy a company whose employees are primarily in a foreign country, the SBIC cannot provide you with a loan or an equity investment. And, you cannot purchase a financial services company with an SBIC loan. There are other rules of the road in dealing with SBICs, and you can read about each of the 300+ SBICs at www.sba.gov/sbic.

Reverse Merger Into Public Shells

A public shell is a public corporation that has no operations, merely some assets, a few liabilities and a lot of stockholders, many of whom, have forgotten they invested in this "piece of doo-doo," or another phrase. A "clean" public shell is a shell that has no assets and no liabilities, but does have a lot of stockholders, many of whom have forgotten that they own the stock. If your desire is to run a publicly-held company, and you currently do not have a company at all, just a desire, you should buy a "clean" public shell. In fact, I cannot imagine why you would "buy trouble."

Shells come about because eager underwriters take companies public before they have proven that they have a product to be manufactured or an idea for a business that can be implemented. So, very weak businesses are foisted on an unknowing public. It happens in cycles; i.e., there are hot IPO markets and there are cold IPO markets. Very weak companies are taken public during hot IPO markets, and as they go bust, the window for future IPOs closes, and stays closed for many months. It is in these times of very few IPOs, or no IPOs, that clean public shells are fairly pricey. When the IPO market is hot, clean public shells are relatively inexpensive.

The solar industry has produced many public shells. Let's say that University Solar Systems, Inc. ("USS") was foisted on an unknowing public with an offering of 6,000,000 shares for $.25 per share, for a $1,500,000 IPO. USS did not commercialize its panels, and its interested customers looked elsewhere for their panels. With $50,000 left in the bank, USS telephones some small investment bankers to see if they will find a buyer for the public-ness of the business and the $50,000 in the bank. The latter begins to dissipate and eventually becomes nothing. No investment banker will take on the task and the CEO of USS runs an ad in the Wall Street Journal that says, "Clean public shell for sale. Small amount of cash. No liabilities. Best offer."

You read the ad, contact the seller and agree to a price of $150,000 for the publicness of a business with no assets, no business plan and no people. Why? Because of its flexibility.

Let's assume that USS has 6,000,000 shares outstanding and the stock is trading every now and then for $0.02 per share. Total shares issued and outstanding are 48,000,000 and you just acquired 42,000,000 of them. You control a publicly-held company. You should operate in stealth mode. No announcement to drive up price. That is a no-no. What you can do to get the stock price up is do a reverse split of 10 for one and the public shareholders now have 600,000 shares trading at $0.20 per share and you have 4,200,000.

You can now seek a seller to acquire via a leveraged buyout. Perhaps you find a wall board manufacturer and distributor in Orlando, FL with sales of $14 million and Adjusted EBITA of $800,000. You can borrow $3,200,000 in the form of a mezzanine loan and you can borrow $1,000,000 on the seller's $1,300,000 of the seller's accounts receivable and $500,000 on finished goods inventory, for an overall borrowing package of $5,000,000. But, the owner wants $6,500,000 and he will not take a seller's note for more than $250,000. How do you close the deal? With a convertible preferred stock, convertible in to USS's common stock at $0.50 per share. But, your stock is trading at $0.20, and that is "by appointment," or occasionally. You go into sales mode: you sell the owner on the upside of the 500,000 shares of USS that you are handing over to him. He has to hold it for at least six months, while a market forms for it. And, he succumbs with, "Well, at least it's a preferred stock, so that is some comfort."

Now, you can announce the acquisition. You can tell the press that USS has acquired a building materials company with sales of $14,000,000 and earnings of $800,000 with financing provided by (names of asset-based and mezzanine lenders). The company is earning 12 cents per share before debt service, and at a multiple of 8.0x, the stock price should move up to somewhere between $.50 and $.90, and it will be your job to keep making acquisitions to justify that price and higher prices. Talk to the press as little as possible, until you have made at least five acquisitions, and are auditing USS's financial statements, and are a fully reporting company. Continue using the convertible preferred stock to make acquisitions, and moving the conversion price up with each leveraged buyout that you complete. The analysts who follow small publicly-held companies will notice the trend, and start to follow USS. If the analysts write up your story, middle market merger and acquisition brokers will begin sending you companies to buy. You could be the reincarnation of Charles Bluhdorn or Henry Singleton. And that, my friends, is Hall of Fame territory.

SPACs – Special Purpose Acquisition Companies

Investment banks such as National Securities Corporation and Jeffries, Inc. raise "blind pools" from wealthy individuals, and file with the SEC for these blind pools to trade publicly. The pools have anywhere from $30 million to $80 million in them. Managers of these pools, like Tina Pappas, known in the trade as the "Queen of SPACs," search for existing companies that have at least $30 million in sales and $5 million in EBITDA to acquire with the publicly-trading shares. It is a means of a company achieving a public market for its shares, or it is an opportunity for a management team that a startup entrepreneur like yourself can cobble together to manage the company once acquired buy the SPAC.

To accomplish that task, let's say you have come out of the U.S. Marines with quite a bit of technical training in armaments, and that the manager of one of the blind pools has found a manufacturer of tactical weapons that is for sale, and the owners want to leave. The match could be perfect. You visit with Ms. Pappas, or another blind pool manager and conduct thorough due diligence on the seller. Although some of the products they sell are a bit antiquated, you and your team believe the new technology that you want to bring matches pretty well with the selling company's customer base. It is very difficult to obtain a vendor number enabling you to sell to the U.S. Department of Defense, and having that, plus a new product line with night vision devices and the ability to see through concrete will be of interest to the selling company's customer base. Or, at least that's the plan.

The negotiations will be interesting. What is a management team with potentially exciting products worth to a SPAC with $50 million in it, of which $30 million is going out the door to the owners of the selling company? You have a couple of cards to play. First, the owners of the selling company are leaving, and a senior management team is needed. That is your Ace in the hole. Your exciting new products are the next best thing, and the third could be that you arrange asset-based loans and mezzanine financing to reduce the amount of cash that the SPAC needs to offer the sellers. Perhaps your team will end up with 33. Anything above 25% ownership would be win in my opinion.

WRAP-UP

It has been an honor and a pleasure to share with you my experiences and information about the myriad and interesting ways for entrepreneurs to fund their start-ups. If I haven't been sufficiently clear on one or more points, or if you want to speak with me about upfront financing for your startup, please feel free to email me at dsilver@sfcapital.com.